THIS BOOK BELONGS TO

CYCLE CODE

1   Remember YOU are responsible for your own safety, and those with you.
2   Keep an eye on youngsters, especially near locks and other danger spots
3   It's wise to carry a small First Aid Kit and puncture repair kit- - I always carry a spare inner tube.
4   Sa...
    yo...
5   Pl...
    a...
6   Do...
    better and carry diseases - -YUK.
7   Don't go too far and get stranded. Make sure you know the relevent Bus and Train Information.
8   Ladies don't go alone - there are some very strange people about.
9   Don't speed on bicycles, dismount in busy areas or near locks and bridges if necessary, and
10 Enjoy yourself.

All maps drawn from OS Series 6 1" to 1 mile 1945-47.

KEY TO MAPS

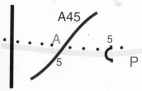

Canal with railway, road and access point, turnover bridge
n.b. An individual rail bridge may be shown

A = Access
S = swapping
P = pub (The Kings Arms)
S = shop

Canal with lock, tunnel, swapping point and towpath shown with dotted line.
n.b. not all bridges are marked for clarity.

INTRODUCTION

The canals of Britain have been described in recent years as linear parks, and that is truly what they are, providing both relaxation with the joy of travel. Each watery route is a complete adventure that gives ever changing vistas of urban and rural landscape. Our canals pass through some of the most beautiful countryside in Britain, but they also visit large thriving cities, jostling market towns and delightful sleepy villages that seem untouched by the passage of time.

Along the towpath you will discover marinas, alive with gaily painted narrowboats, marvellous pieces of architecture, wild birds and flowers, enormous dragonflies, and if you are lucky the glorious flash from a kingfisher. You'll just wish you had discovered our marvellous inland waterway system before.

The canals themselves along with the towpath, locks and other accessories are cared for in the main by British Waterways, though much work has been done by canal societies and local authorities. Walkers do not need a permit but cyclists do. At the moment there is a free permit for the majority of waterways, and a charged permit for the Kennet and Avon, both available from BW. However the policy on permits can and probably will change, so it's worth ringing BW for the latest info TEL 01923 226081

THE TOWPATH

Towpath conditions vary from wonderful to poor, so you need to see the relevent page for details, photographs have been included where appropriate. However at this stage I must make a point about the Grand Union. The week that I decided to cycle this canal I encountered gangs of men along most of it's length digging it up. They were in the process of laying a green tube that is to house a fibre optic cable. This cable I was told is, to give more impetus to the world of communication (as if we need it?) I was also informed that the condition of the towpath should be better after the work is finished than it was before. Therefore we live in hope. Sadly this may make some of my comments on the state of the path out of date before

they are printed. What a frustrating world we live in eh?. Still I have a card up my sleeve in the shape of a roving reporter, who promises to ring me up from his boat and give me the latest details, so maybe my work is not in vain? So yes it is possible to go on a journey of discovery and exploration in 20th century Britain, and the modes of transport are the best of all, by foot or by bicycle. Walking is a most pleasant form of travel, especially with friends, and it gives you the most time to savour the views, but it is quite slow. Cycling to my mind is the most enjoyable of all, and your bike becomes your trusty (or in some cases rusty) companion. Lets face it the bikes got to be one of the best things man has ever invented.

Cycling itself is continuing to gain great popularity, not just amongst the young but also with older people who are seeking a gentle form of exercise, and the canal towpath is a marvellous place due to it's generally flat surface. British Waterways are only recently coming to grips with what to do with cyclists, having over the years an on off affair with the permit scheme.

Personally I am all in favour of a sensible and reasonable cycling permit that will benefit BW and go toward needed maintenance for the towpath and I look forward to seeing it finally

and nationally sorted out. But at this point I would like to thank the British Waterways staff for being

approachable and helpful in compiling these maps.

So if your looking for adventure, inspiration or relaxation, and avoid all the anxieties that come with jetting off to Spain, why not sample the hidden delights of Britain and it's historic inland waterway system.

The good thing is you can do as little or as much as you like, and when you like. Each person or group of people will walk or cycle at their own pace, and you will have to discover yours. I have cycled every inch of these routes and simply loved the experience, but my pace is leisurely, around 25-30 miles per day. This gives me the opportunity to look around, enjoy the scenery, take a few photographs or even do a sketch. Then there are the pubs to visit, and I have noticed that all the best pubs are to be found right on the canal side. Not only do they supply the obvious requirements of rest, food and drink, they also serve as navigational points along the way. My travelling philosophy is therefore, we need to know three things in life, where we are, where we came from, and most importantly where the next pub is.

THE CANAL SYSTEM- ROUTES AND ACCOMMODATION

Our inland waterway system is wonderful and amazing , in labour terms it compares to the building of the pyramids. Created during the industrial revolution to provide a cheap and efficient means of transporting vast quantities of goods and materials, it went into decline after the advent of the railways, and finally became redundant when the remainder of its work went to the lorry. Then in the first half of the twentieth century it went through a difficult period when many local and national authorities either ignored it's potential or worse tried to get rid of it, and many miles of canal were infact filled in and in some cases built over.

Fortunately, due to the efforts of certain individuals and canal societies (see Changing Roles) they have been saved and given a new lease of life. We can be certain that none of the original canal promoters like Josiah Wedgewood or James Watt could ever have dreamed that their canals would at some future time become a total leisure facility. But that is exactly what has happened, and people are coming from all parts of the world to enjoy this unique experience.

Because the routes in this book range from quite long to extremely long, ie The Grand Union, Birmingham to London canal is around one hundred and fifty miles, it's pretty obvious that they need to be done in stages. This means deciding how far you or your group are going to travel in one day (without biting off more than you can chew) and then have accommodation waiting, or some form of transport to take you home. I have included in the notes a couple of places where I have had or spotted B&B, but it makes sense to use an accommodation guide. British Waterways have a useful booklet which contains places to stay along The Grand Union, which can be obtained from them, or from such places as The Stop House Braunston.

It is also sensible to arrange your accommodation in advance, this will save you the stress of scouring villages at the end of the day when you are already tired from your exertions, believe me I've done it, sometimes it works out ok but not always.

CYCLING

For the most part cyclists do not need to be hardened veterans, but it is worth pointing out that many miles of towpath are still much as they were a hundred years ago, and have received little or no maintenance, and therefore

require a degree of cycling skill. Don't forget the canal though not terribly deep is never far away, and even though I personally have never fallen in, I know a man that has. Having said that, I admit to teaching my daughter to cycle by using the canal towpath from an early age. I held the view that I would rather have my little girl fall into two feet of water, with me close at hand, than go under the wheels of a ten ton truck. Obviously there is always need for caution, especially when near locks where the water is considerably deeper (see cycle code) But it's good to see family groups out discovering canal routes, exercising a little wisdom and having an enjoyable time.

IMPORTANT NOTE

Not all towpaths are cyclable due to their condition, and it is the purpose of the key map for each canal to point out the sections that British Waterways regard as unsuitable at present for cycling. However new sections are being upgraded all the time, so the future looks bright, and it will be even better if walkers and cyclists alike take good care of the facilities available. Also don't forget that moneys paid for cycling permits will all add to further improvements.

EQUIPMENT

An expensive bike is not required, but it does need to be well maintained and checked over before embarking on a long ride. I have found that rear panniers are wonderful for storing all manner of things including waterproofs, food and drink. Then there is the need to take along a few basic tools, a puncture repair outfit and a spare inner tube. Sometimes British Waterways guys cut the hawthorn hedges that line the towpath, and the carelessly left clippings can lead to serious deflation problems, causing long delays. Fitting nylon inserts to your tyres is a good idea and works well. Other towpath users often complain that cyclists never have a bell, so I would encourage you at this point to fit one and use it.

CIRCULAR ROUTES

Canals often go through quiet country areas, where there are only villages served by less frequented B roads. Due to the scale of the maps it is possible to show these, and they have been drawn half the thickness of the more busy A roads. These country lanes often run parallel with the canal, even crossing it at intervals and they can be linked with the towpath to create interesting circular routes varying in length from five or six miles to over twenty. Examples of these trips can be found on pages 14, between Lapworth and Warwick. 17 between Leamington Spa and Long Itchington. Pages 18/19 between Napton and Braunston (see text). Page 20 between Weedon Bec and Gayton Junction. Pages 34/35 between Marston Doles and Wormleighton and between Claydon, Cropredy and Little Bourton. Pages 36/37 around Kings Sutton and Lower Heyford, though other rides on these pages can be made by using the A4260 through Deddington if your used to busier roads- WITH HILLS, I must add. Pages 48/49 in the superb cycling Vale of Pewsey, utilising the Wiltshire Cycle Way. Pages 50/51 between Wootton Rivers and Kintbury, pages 52 and 53, between Woolhampton and Kintbury, via the villages of Brimpton, Greenham and Hamstead Marshall.

THE BEST BITS

Due to the hard going on some towpaths, ie where it is grassy, I have selected certain sections from the main routes and labelled them **THE BEST BITS** . I have categorised them such for the following reasons.

1. The towpath is in very good condition, wide enough and firm enough for easy cycling and walking .
2. The countryside is particularly attractive.
3. There may be historical or architectural features of interest
4. They are especially suitable for families. and finally
5. I liked them

OXFORD CANAL

MARSTON DOLES TO FENNY COMPTON 10 AND A HALF MILES

The towpath on this section has been dramatically improved by the addition of an orange gravel layer, making it a good surface for walkers and cyclists. Please note however that there are no pubs or shops on this bit, so you will need to carry your own refreshments. By examining the map you will notice that the road to Priors Hardwick makes a circular route of approx 16 miles.

CROPREDY TO BANBURY 4 AND A HALF MILES

This route takes you from one extreme to the other, from the bustling market town of Banbury to the attractive sleepy village of Cropredy. After leaving the M40 behind there are three wonderful miles of towpath punctuated by two locks just to break things up.Cropredy has a connection with the English civil war of the 1640s (you know, the one between King Charles and Cromwell) and a battle was fought near here.

OXFORD TO THE ROCK OF GIBRALTER PUB 9 AND A HALF MILES

An excellent towpath with plenty of nice pubs on the way. The Boat at Thrupp was in the process of being rebuilt when I passed last, but a friendly builder informed me that it would be finished by the autumn of 97. The Jolly Boatman close by on the A423 is wedged securely between road and canal and does a variety of meals, and there is excellent access to the canal at this point.

KENNET & AVON

BATH TO DEVIZES 23 MILES

The twenty three miles between these interesting towns must be amongst the most beautiful and spectacular stretches in the whole book, and includes scenic views in the Bradford on Avon and Bathampton areas. The towpath is simply a delight, wide, rolled and gritted, making it perfect for family walking or cycling. The bike shop in Bradford on Avon does hiring and repairs of bikes, phone no at the back.

INTRODUCTION TO THE GRAND UNION CANAL

Back in the 1750s there was no M40, and no M1, therefore if you wanted to travel to London from Birmingham it would have been a long arduous trip, over rough terrain, on even rougher roads. The transportation of goods of any quantity was even worse.

The birth of the true transport canal came in the 1760s, when the Bridgewater canal was opened near Manchester to shift the Dukes coal from his mines at Worsley. From then on it seemed that canals were being dug everywhere, and by the 1790s there was a route by water between the capital and the rapidly developing second city. This passage however was an extremely long way round, going north east from Birmingham to Fazeley, then down the Oxford canal, and then finally along the Thames. Therefore a more direct route was desired, an initial survey being undertaken in 1792 by James Barnes of Banbury and commissioned by the Marquis of Bath.

William Jessop did a later survey, and agreed with the earlier findings of Barnes on the route he had advised. Jessop eventually became the chief engineer for the line, with Barnes also serving as engineer. The Grand Junction canal as it was then known, was started like all others by an act of parliament in 1793 and was to run from Braunston to Brentford, with additional arms. That year also saw the plans for a link between Warwick and Birmingham, which itself was extended to Napton.

From the outset, the Grand Junction was planned as a wider than usual waterway, in order that larger cargoes could be carried on barges instead of the usual 70foot x 7 foot narrow boats that were limited by size to around thirty tons. But because there was no national policy for the canal system, the individual canal companies being in direct competition with each other, behaved like spoiled school boys, and their self interest and constant squabbling prevented any unified scheme as far as canal width was concerned.

The Grand Junction was opened in sections, as some areas were held back from finishing by constructional problems, especially where long tunnels were being built, ie Blissworth. The whole length was up and running by 1805, which must have been an exciting period in British history when you remember that we were at war with Napoleon and the French (after just losing to the Americans). Infact the battle of Trafalgar was fought in 1805. And of course dear old Jane Austen was writing Pride and Prejudice so that we could watch it on the Beeb nearly 200 years later. So if you were a young fit man in those days and were poor, you could either have been shot by the French, shot by the Yanks or worked to death on the canals.

Until the railways came in the 1840s, the canals did a roaring trade, moving everything from fresh farm produce to iron and coal, but the much faster rail service brought a reduction in trade, and the motor lorry used extensively between the two world wars, coupled with an improved road network finally brought about its demise.

In 1929 the Regents Canal Co acquired the Grand Junction and the Warwick canals and formed (you've guessed) The Grand Union. There was a degree of improvement work carried out but certainly no resurrection to it's former glory, that is of course until pleasure boating became popular. So if your starting your journey either by boat or by foot and commence at the centre of Birmingham (which I hasten to add is now a most attractive city, especially around the canal area) and head down the thirteen locks to Aston Junction, and finish at Brentford High Street, then you will have done about a hundred and forty one miles, passed one hundred and seventy locks and had a marvellous time in the process.

THE GRAND UNION CANAL
Birmingham to Brentford 141 miles 170 locks.

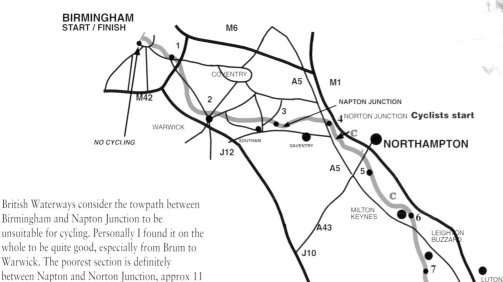

BIRMINGHAM
START / FINISH

M6

COVENTRY

A5

M1

M42

WARWICK

NO CYCLING

SOUTHAM

DAVENTRY

J12

A5

NAPTON JUNCTION

NORTON JUNCTION **Cyclists start**

NORTHAMPTON

MILTON KEYNES

A43

J10

LEIGHTON BUZZARD

M40

IVINGHOE

TRING

WENDOVER

HIGH WYCOMBE

LUTON

M25

LONDON

BRENTFORD
START / FINISH

British Waterways consider the towpath between Birmingham and Napton Junction to be unsuitable for cycling. Personally I found it on the whole to be quite good, especially from Brum to Warwick. The poorest section is definitely between Napton and Norton Junction, approx 11 miles, and the maps on pages 18, 19 show an alternative off and on road route. SO if you want to miss all of this out, then the ideal start point for cyclists must be Norton Junction. See page 19 for access.

N.B. Some books show a total of 147 miles, but 141 is what I clocked with my trusty cycle computer, so that's what I'm sticking to. All I can say is , you do it and see what you get?

Birmingham to Kingswood Junction	16 miles (1)
Kingswood Junction to Warwick	8 miles (2)
Warwick to Bridge 21 (The Boat)	11 miles (3)
Bridge 21 to Norton junction	13.5 miles (4)
Norton Junction to Blisworth	14 miles (5)
Blisworth to Milton Keynes (bridge 90)	18 miles (6)
Milton Keynes (B90) to Bridge 12	17 miles (7)
Bridge 123(Cheddington) to B155	15 miles (8)
Bridge 155 to the A40 (Denham)	15.5 miles (9)
Denham (A40) to Brentford	13 miles

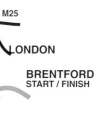

BIRMINGHAM TO KINGSWOOD JUNCTION
16 miles

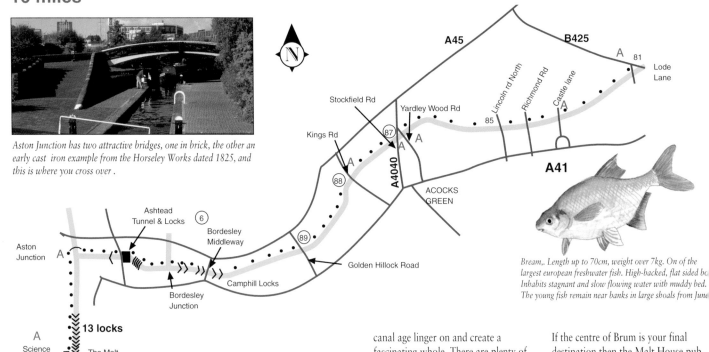

Aston Junction has two attractive bridges, one in brick, the other an early cast iron example from the Horseley Works dated 1825, and this is where you cross over .

Bream,. Length up to 70cm, weight over 7kg. On of the largest european freshwater fish. High-backed, flat sided bo. Inhabits stagnant and slow flowing water with muddy bed. The young fish remain near banks in large shoals from June

Birmingham has gone through great changes over the last few years with lots of new attractive buildings like Symphony Hall and the Indoor Arena, however some remnants of the canal age linger on and create a fascinating whole. There are plenty of access points , for example off Broad st, or at the Science Museum. At Farmers Bridge Junction sits The Malt House Pub and it's just over a mile from here to Aston Junction when you turn right and head for Warwick.

If the centre of Brum is your final destination then the Malt House pub is the perfect place to celebrate, revive your spirits, take a seat and watch the world go by. If this is the start of your trek, what are you waiting for? Get those legs going Nort to Aston Junction.

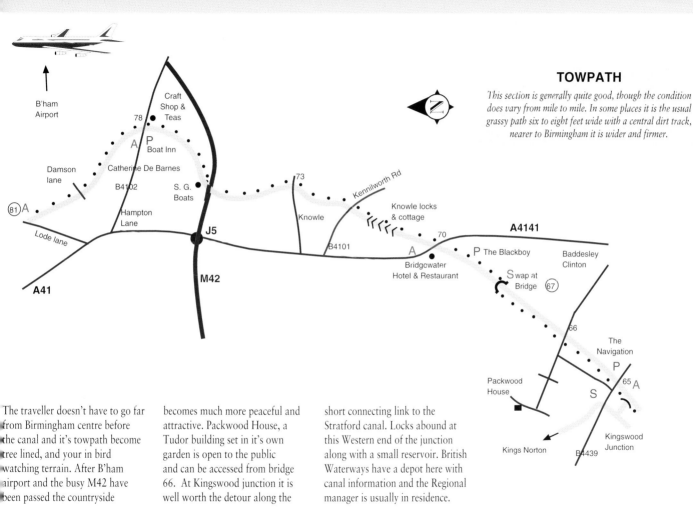

TOWPATH

This section is generally quite good, though the condition does vary from mile to mile. In some places it is the usual grassy path six to eight feet wide with a central dirt track, nearer to Birmingham it is wider and firmer.

B'ham Airport

Craft Shop & Teas

78

A P Boat Inn

Damson lane

Catherine De Barnes

B4102

S. G. Boats

81 A

Hampton Lane

Lode lane

A41

J5

M42

73

Knowle

B4101

Kennilworth Rd

Knowle locks & cottage

70

A

Bridgewater Hotel & Restaurant

A4141

P The Blackboy

Baddesley Clinton

S wap at Bridge

67

66

The Navigation

P

65 A

Packwood House

S

Kings Norton

B4439

Kingswood Junction

The traveller doesn't have to go far from Birmingham centre before the canal and it's towpath become tree lined, and your in bird watching terrain. After B'ham airport and the busy M42 have been passed the countryside becomes much more peaceful and attractive. Packwood House, a Tudor building set in it's own garden is open to the public and can be accessed from bridge 66. At Kingswood junction it is well worth the detour along the short connecting link to the Stratford canal. Locks abound at this Western end of the junction along with a small reservoir. British Waterways have a depot here with canal information and the Regional manager is usually in residence.

KINGSWOOD JUNCTION TO WARWICK
8 miles 21 locks. + Circular Route

TOWPATH

Good throughout and the route goes through some beautiful countryside. Kingswood Junction is a pleasant spot to linger and maybe have a picnic. It is an unusual and interesting location with plenty of locks and a short stretch of canal that forms the link between the Stratford and Grand Union Canal.

B'ham

P The Navigation
65

Kings Norton

A

Kingswood
Junction

A

Tom 'O'
The Wood

P

Rowington

62

A

B4439

A4177

Hatton

55

Yacht Club

Shrewley
Common

A

Stratford

M40

S P

56

Tunnel of 396m
Follow track over top

The Hatton lock system with it's reedy side ponds must have proved a weary sight to the approaching narrow boat crew. Nevertheless it also gives us one of the most amazing and dramatic prospects as the canal climbs up a little over 146 feet through a total of 21 chambers.

Shrewley tunnel is typical, having no towpath through its length and boats were apparently propelled along by rails that were set into the walls. The path over the top is as clear as you can get, and there is a shop not far from where the track and road intersect at the top.

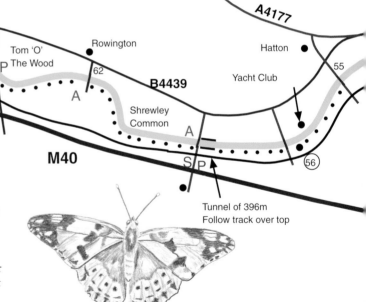

Painted lady

Warwick Castle.

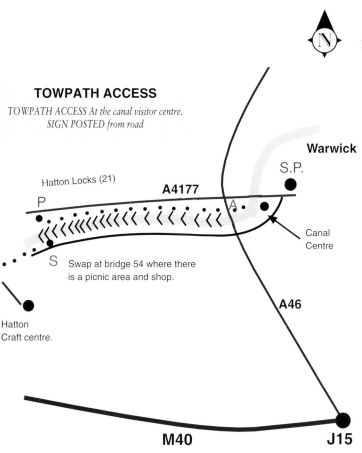

TOWPATH ACCESS

TOWPATH ACCESS At the canal visitor centre.
SIGN POSTED from road

N

Hatton Locks (21)

A4177

Warwick

S.P.

P

A

Canal
Centre

S   Swap at bridge 54 where there
is a picnic area and shop.

A46

Hatton
Craft centre.

M40   **J15**

The early town was founded as a primitive fortification right next to the river Avon in AD 914 by Ethelfleda, sister of Edward the Elder, and daughter of Alfred the Great. Ethelfledas greatest concern was from bands of marauding Danes who at this time in Englands history were invading central areas and utilising rivers like the Avon and Severn as their version of the M1. In medieval times most of the buildings were constructed from oak frames with wattle and daub infill. Due to the combustible nature of this material many structures were sadly lost in the great fire of 1694. Fortunately not all were destroyed, and some were replaced in the attractive styles of the late 17th early 18th century, producing a pleasant mix of architectural themes.

Warwick is a splendid historic town to spend time in, and the castle has got to be one of the best preserved examples of its kind, hosting a wide variety of functions.

Hatton Country World is a mix of leisure and shopping facility. The village has 25 craft and gift shops, and is open from 10 am till 5.30. It is sign posted off the A4177 and then crossing bridge 55.

WARWICK CANAL CENTRE TO THE BOAT PUB
11 miles 22 locks. + Circular Route B34 - B27 or the Blue Lias

Lord Leycester Hospital and West Gate.
An absolutely fabulous timber framed building, dating from the fourteenth century and open to visitors. It contains guildhall and museum of Queens own Hussars, and was founded in 1571 by Robert Dudley Earl of Leicester for the poor. Today it serves as a home for retired or disabled serviceman. As for Pride and Prejudice viewers it was used in the TV adaptation with Colin Firth and Jennifer Ehle.

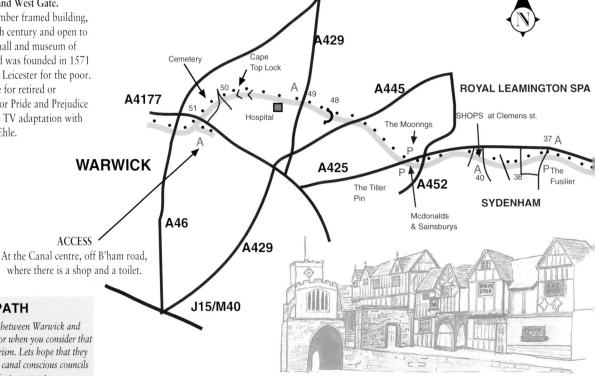

Cemetery

Cape Top Lock

A429

50

51

A4177

A

49

48

A445

ROYAL LEAMINGTON SPA

Hospital

SHOPS at Clemens st.

The Moorings

WARWICK

37 A

A

P

A425

P

A

40

38

P The Fusilier

The Tiller Pin

A452

SYDENHAM

A46

Mcdonalds & Sainsburys

ACCESS
At the Canal centre, off B'ham road, where there is a shop and a toilet.

A429

J15/M40

TOWPATH
The path on this section between Warwick and Leamington Spa is quite poor when you consider that both towns encourage tourism. Lets hope that they take the lesson from more canal conscious councils and make some improvements.

Lord Leycester Hospital.

Leaving Warwick behind.

20 locks on this page alone, many of which were renewed in the 1920s. Although presenting plenty of work to the poor narrow boat crew they pose little problem to the walker or cyclist. However they do serve as excellent navigational markers along the way.

The Blue Lias is named after the blue grey limestone that used to be quarried in this area for the cement industry.

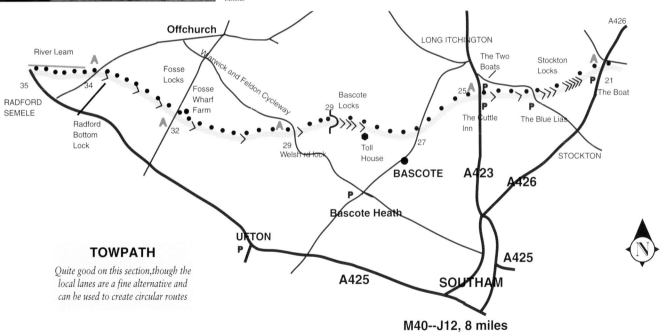

Offchurch

River Leam

35

RADFORD SEMELE

34

Radford Bottom Lock

32

Fosse Locks

Fosse Wharf Farm

Warwick and Feldon Cycleway

29 Welsh rd lock

Bascote Locks

29

27

Toll House

BASCOTE

Bascote Heath

P

UFTON

P

LONG ITCHINGTON

The Two Boats

25

The Cuttle Inn

Stockton Locks

The Blue Lias

A426

The Boat

21

STOCKTON

A423

A426

A425

SOUTHAM

A425

M40--J12, 8 miles

TOWPATH

Quite good on this section, though the local lanes are a fine alternative and can be used to create circular routes

N

17

BRIDGE 21 (THE BOAT) TO NORTON JUNCTION
13½ miles 9 locks. + Circular Route

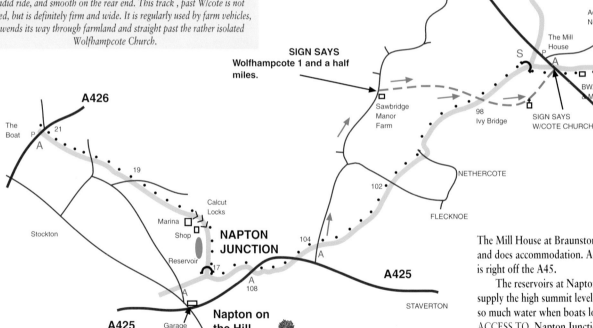

SIGN SAYS
Wolfhampcote 1 and a half miles.

SIGN SAYS
W/COTE CHURCH

WILLOUGHBY

A45

BRAUNSTON

Admiral Nelson

The Mill House

Road to Welton

S P A

Crafts

BW. office, shop & Marina

Top Lock

A45

Sawbridge Manor Farm

98
Ivy Bridge

NETHERCOTE

102

FLECKNOE

A426

The Boat P 21
A

19

Stockton

Calcut Locks

Marina

Shop

Reservoir

NAPTON JUNCTION

17

104
A

A
108

A425

STAVERTON

A
A425 Garage

Napton on the Hill

The Mill House at Braunston is a huge affair, and does accommodation. Access to the canal is right off the A45.

The reservoirs at Napton were built to supply the high summit level, that loses so much water when boats lock up and down. ACCESS TO Napton Junction is by following the road down the side of the Murco Garage t the Marina.

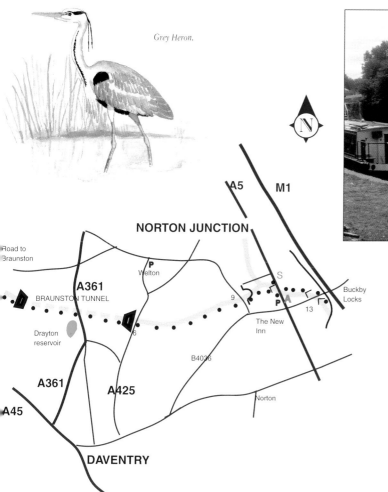

Grey Heron.

N

A5   M1

NORTON JUNCTION

Road to Braunston

P
Welton

A361
BRAUNSTON TUNNEL

S

9

Buckby Locks

P A

13

The New Inn

Drayton reservoir

6

B4036

A361

A425

Norton

A45

DAVENTRY

Calcutt Locks and Marina

BRAUNSTON TUNNEL

Just follow the track over the top, it's easy enough, though the eastern end is a little overgrown. When the canal was being built, Braunston tunnel proved to be much more difficult to dig out than Blissworth, and ended up with a double kink along it's length due to the poor workmanship of the engineer, who had his pay halved for his error. The tunnel was finally opened on the 21st June 1796.

TOWPATH

There are a few eroded bits between bridge 6 and 9. Cyclists can as an alternative go through Braunston and rejoin the canal at bridge 9. ACCESS to Norton Junction is off J17/M1 and down the A5.

NORTON JUNCTION TO BLISWORTH
14 miles 6 locks. + Circular Route B29 - Gayton

TOWPATH

Reasonably clear, with a firm central track. After running East from Brum for several miles, at Norton J it does a 90 degree turn , and finally heads South.

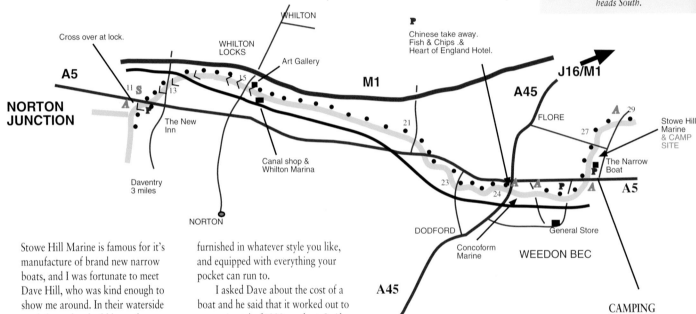

Stowe Hill Marine is famous for it's manufacture of brand new narrow boats, and I was fortunate to meet Dave Hill, who was kind enough to show me around. In their waterside workshops they build boats from scratch, usually to order. At one end of the shed arrives the sheet steel at 10mm and 6mm thickness, and six months later out pops another treasured craft. I discovered that during the building process you can have it finished and furnished in whatever style you like, and equipped with everything your pocket can run to.

I asked Dave about the cost of a boat and he said that it worked out to approximately £1000 per foot. So if you ordered a 65 foot boat, then the bill would be about £65000- - easy isn't it? Please note though that there is a two year waiting list (It will give you time to save your pennies up.)

CAMPING
at Millar Marine, next to the pub,rig the A5. The camp site is on the canal and is quite a nice spot, though there no toilet facilities at the moment. TEL 01327 349188

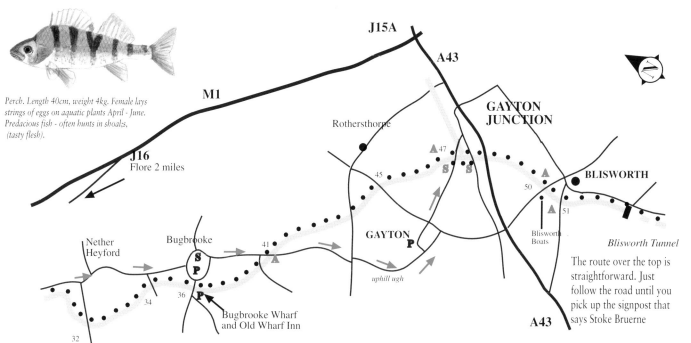

Perch. Length 40cm, weight 4kg. Female lays strings of eggs on aquatic plants April - June. Predacious fish - often hunts in shoal;s, (tasty flesh).

M1

J15A

A43

GAYTON JUNCTION

Rothersthorpe

J16
Flore 2 miles

▲47

45

S S

BLISWORTH

50

▲

GAYTON
P

▲ 51

Blisworth Boats

uphill ugh

A43

Blisworth Tunnel

The route over the top is straightforward. Just follow the road until you pick up the signpost that says Stoke Bruerne

Nether Heyford

Bugbrooke

S
P
P

41
▲

34

36
P

32

Bugbrooke Wharf and Old Wharf Inn

TOWPATH

Typical G/U, wide enough in most parts, perfect for walking but a little hard going for cycling. A splendid alternative is the route marked with green arrows that goes along quiet country lanes and passes the small sleepy villages of Nether Heyford, Bugbrooke and Gayton. Or both canal towpath and roads can be used to make great circular trips by using the access points off bridges 27 or 29, Gayton Junction or Blisworth. Bugbrooke is the largest of the villages and has a useful, well stocked general store.

Heading East toward Norton Junction

21

BLISWORTH TO BRIDGE 90 (A421)
18 miles 8 locks.

Stoke Bruerne is an extremely popular spot for boaters and day trippers alike, who come in hordes on a summers day to enjoy the canal side experience. Not only does the place boast a fine Museum, there is also a well stocked bookshop, two pubs, cafe and boat trips into the blackness of Blisworth tunnel. Its simply a gongoozlers paradise, and easily accessed from J 15\M1, and down the A508.

The museum provides a fascinating and colourful insight into a transport system that was of paramount importance to the development of the industrial revolution. There are working models, videos and displays portraying every aspect of the working history of the waterways. TEL 01604 862229.

Alan Faulkner in his book The Grand Junction Canal, give us an interesting snippet of information from the days when steam tugs were employed to pull craft through the tunnel. Due to the thick layers of soot that built up on the roof and walls, a special boat with bristles on handles was dragged all the way through to remove the build up. It must have been a horrible task for the men who did it. It made me wonder how the job was advertised, ' Horizontal Chimney Sweep required' ?

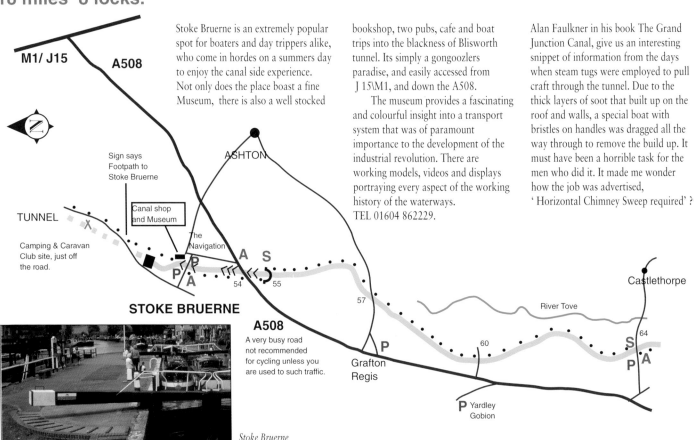

M1/ J15

A508

ASHTON

Sign says
Footpath to
Stoke Bruerne

Canal shop
and Museum

TUNNEL

Camping & Caravan
Club site, just off
the road.

The
Navigation

P A S

STOKE BRUERNE

A508
A very busy road
not recommended
for cycling unless you
are used to such traffic.

54   55

57

Grafton
Regis

P

Yardley
Gobion

P

60

River Tove

Castlethorpe

64

S
P A

Stoke Bruerne

22

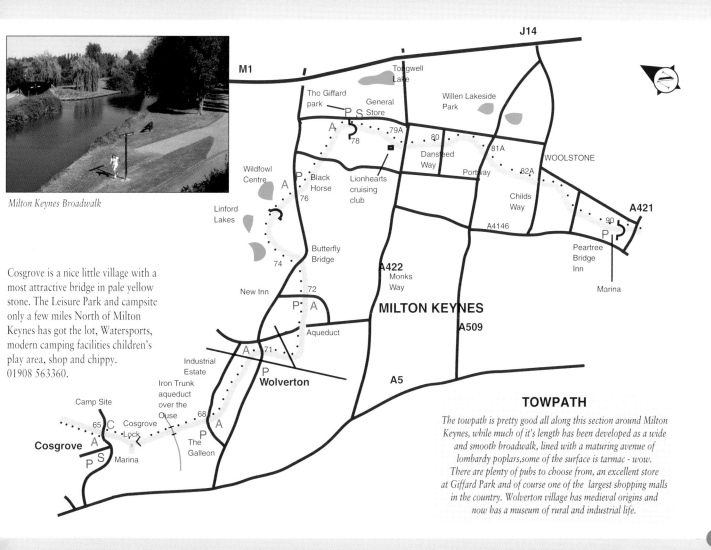

Milton Keynes Broadwalk

Cosgrove is a nice little village with a most attractive bridge in pale yellow stone. The Leisure Park and campsite only a few miles North of Milton Keynes has got the lot, Watersports, modern camping facilities children's play area, shop and chippy. 01908 563360.

J14

M1

Tongwell Lake

The Giffard park

General Store

P S

A

78

79A

80

Danseed Way

Willen Lakeside Park

81A

WOOLSTONE

82A

Portway

A421

Wildfowl Centre

P A

Black Horse

76

Lionhearts cruising club

Childs Way

90

P

Linford Lakes

A4146

Peartree Bridge Inn

Butterfly Bridge

74

A422

Monks Way

Marina

New Inn

72

P A

MILTON KEYNES

Aqueduct

A509

Wolverton

A

71

P

A5

Industrial Estate

Iron Trunk aqueduct over the Ouse

68

A

Camp Site

65

C

Cosgrove Lock

Cosgrove

P S

Marina

The Galleon

TOWPATH

The towpath is pretty good all along this section around Milton Keynes, while much of it's length has been developed as a wide and smooth broadwalk, lined with a maturing avenue of lombardy poplars, some of the surface is tarmac - wow. There are plenty of pubs to choose from, an excellent store at Giffard Park and of course one of the largest shopping malls in the country. Wolverton village has medieval origins and now has a museum of rural and industrial life.

BRIDGE 90 (MILTON KEYNES) TO BRIDGE 123
17 miles 12 locks.

After enjoying the fresh, new, look of Milton Keynes, which is making the most of it's association with the much older canal, I made my way south. The countryside opened up and became a touch lonely as the towpath wound

it's way through four or five miles of public parkland with the river Ouzel running parallel, until finally Soulbury locks came into view. The Towpath was wide and grassy, but in the process of being dug up. Tesco's who seem to have

an affinity for setting their stores next to the GU were building a huge warehouse at Fenny Stratford, but are thankfully landscaping the surrounding area so that the quiet ambience of the spot is not completely lost .

Blue Tit.

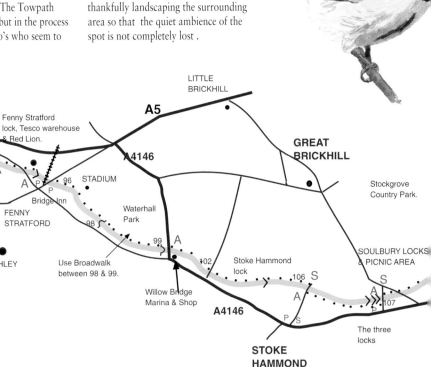

Cowslip.

Leighton Buzzard is a fine historic town, surrounded by its old sandpits, and is easily accessed from the canal by the huge Tesco store. The towpath is pretty good throughout and the occasional solitary lock punctuates the general rural wandering of the canal. The river Ouzel runs parallel to the North. Church lock gets its name from a small former church that is now a private residence. The Globe Inn at Linslade sports a country cottage look, and is perfectly placed for a pint at the waters edge, with a nice view toward the next bridge.

Fenny Stratford Lock.

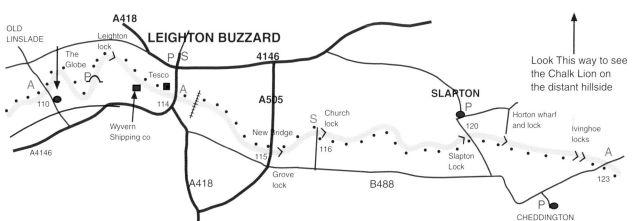

OLD LINSLADE

A418

Leighton lock

LEIGHTON BUZZARD

P S

4146

The Globe

P

A

Tesco

110

114

Wyvern Shipping co

A4146

A418

A505

New Bridge

115

Grove lock

S

Church lock

116

B488

Slapton Lock

SLAPTON

P

120

Horton wharf and lock

Ivinghoe locks

A

123

P

CHEDDINGTON

Look This way to see the Chalk Lion on the distant hillside

BRIDGE 123 (CHEDDINGTON) TO BRIDGE 155 (HEMEL HEMPSTEAD)

15 miles 35 locks.

Lots of interest for the canal traveller on this section with locks, wharves, junctions and cuttings

The reservoir at Marsworth is a popular venue for anglers, and I was pleased to see the majority of them using conventional rods instead of the increasingly popular roach pole which blocks the towpath for walkers and cyclists alike. The fishermen were out to catch the carp, perch, roach and gudgeon that ply the gloomy depths between the groups of locks.

The Cowroast pub is a seventeenth century inn built on a former Roman settlement. The name probably derives from cow rest. In times gone by this would have been a regular stopping point as herds of cattle were transported from the Midlands to London. The present pub does an interesting menu and their telephone no is 01442 822287.

There are an attractive group of buildings here, including a square tower, that serve as a depot for British Waterways.

CHEDDINGTON

B488

123

Seabrooke locks

Grebe canal cruises

PITSTONE GREEN

126

Boat club

TOWPATH

This Northern end has quite a reasonable path, well used and firm. Tring cutting is a deep cool, leafy corridor , with the path swapping sides regularly at B 131, 132 and 138.

B489

Red lion

130 P

A

S

131

S

132

P

White lion

Bulbourne Junction

Tring cutting

133

134

135

Station

P

Grand Junction Arms & picnic area

S

Reservoir & Nature reserve.

MARSWORTH JUNCTION

Craft shop & Tea room

Marina

S

138

136

A4251

137

Cowroast

A

TRING

A41

Two major towns on this section, both can be accessed easily from the canal for those wishing to purchase provisions. Hemel Hempstead is only Two and a half miles from J8 of the M1. **TRING CUTTING** It was at this point that the canal engineers faced the enormous task of taking the canal through the rising ground of the Chilterns. The excavation required a depth of around thirty feet, and a length up to a mile and a half. This was a huge amount of soil and rock to remove with the basic tools of the day, and the question is where do you put it when you've dug it out? As the work progressed the banks were continually giving way, and the extra digging of drainage channels became necessary to remove excess spring water that welled up from below. The Three Horshoes is an Olde Worlde, cottage style country pub, and there is a sad story from the christmas of 1898 when the resident lock keeper from next door, fell into his own lock and drowned after visiting the pub for a few drinky's. There may be a moral to this tale, but for the life of me I can't think what it is.

Peacock Butterfly.

TOWPATH

A wide firm path,excellent for walking, a little bumpy for cyclists after the pipelayers have back filled their trench. The surface is also made up of a sharp type of gravel which hopefully will bed down with use.

Three pubs within a stones throw from each other. Left to right.
The Crystal Palace
The Boat
The Rising Sun

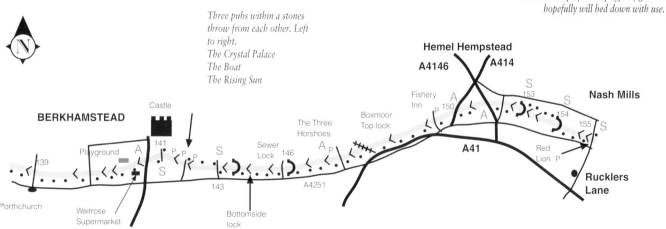

BRIDGE 155 (NASH MILLS) TO THE A40
15½ miles 21 locks.

Just North of Watford, the Grand Junction Canal (as it was formerly known) was destined to go through Cassiobury Park and Grove Park respectively, belonging to the Earls of Essex and Clarendon. The Earl of Essex said that the £10,000 that he had been offered to allow this was not enough, so he held out for another five grand, and got it (well he would wouldn't he?) Both Earls also requested that the canal should be made to look as ornamental as possible, hence the unnecessary meandering river like course, and the addition of an extremely attractive bridge (see The Grove Bridge,164)

TOWPATH *(Northern section)*

Generally a wide firm towpath, great for walking, and not too bad for cycling either, though the surface can be bumpy in places and contains that sharp gravel,so make sure that your tyres are in good order.

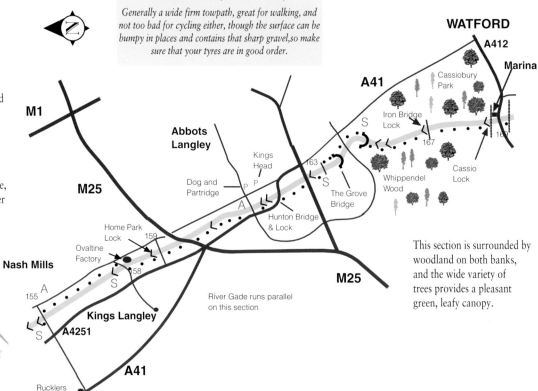

N

M1

M25

Nash Mills

155
A

S

A4251

Rucklers
Lane

A41

Kings Langley

Ovaltine
Factory

Home Park
Lock

158
S

159

River Gade runs parallel
on this section

M25

Abbots
Langley

Dog and
Partridge

P

Kings
Head

P

A

Hunton Bridge
& Lock

The Grove
Bridge

163

S

A41

S

Iron Bridge
Lock

167

WATFORD

A412

Marina

Cassiobury
Park

Whippendel
Wood

Cassio
Lock

16?

This section is surrounded by woodland on both banks, and the wide variety of trees provides a pleasant green, leafy canopy.

Kingfisher.

28

Stockers lock has a pretty cottage next to it, whose owner keeps a rather unusual array of tools. Herons are a regular sight along this section, and sometimes they stand so still you wonder whether they are for real. There is a rather useful B&b only 5 minutes walk from Common Moor lock. 30 Hazelwood rd, Croxley green, 01923 226666.

Rosebay willow herb.

TOWPATH (Northern section)

Is reasonable throughout, wide and generally firm, but wouldn't say no to a little maintenance. Next to the path lie a succession of pools surrounded by lush vegetation that extend all the way from Rickmansworth to Denham, which can be seen in glimpses through the line of trees that screen them from the canal. Denham lock has a rise and fall of eleven feet which makes it the deepest chamber on the Grand Union

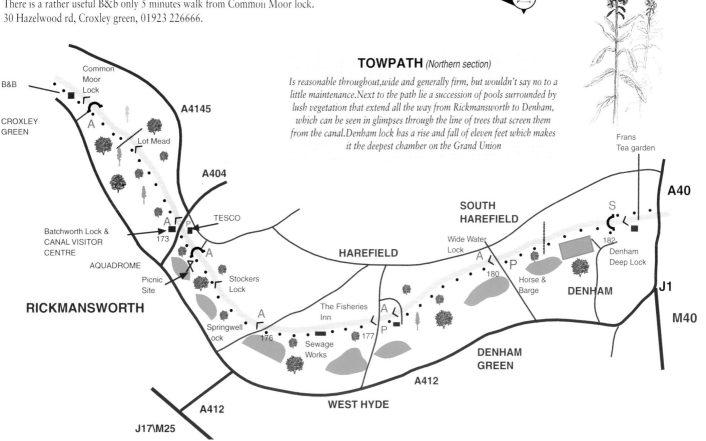

B&B

Common Moor Lock

CROXLEY GREEN

A4145

Lot Mead

A404

A

TESCO

173

Batchworth Lock & CANAL VISITOR CENTRE

AQUADROME

A

Picnic Site

Stockers Lock

RICKMANSWORTH

Springwell lock

A

176

Sewage Works

The Fisheries Inn

A P

177

HAREFIELD

SOUTH HAREFIELD

Wide Water Lock

A

180

P

Horse & Barge

DENHAM

S

182

Denham Deep Lock

Frans Tea garden

A40

J1

M40

DENHAM GREEN

A412

WEST HYDE

A412

J17\M25

M40/A40 TO BRENTFORD
13 miles 12 locks.

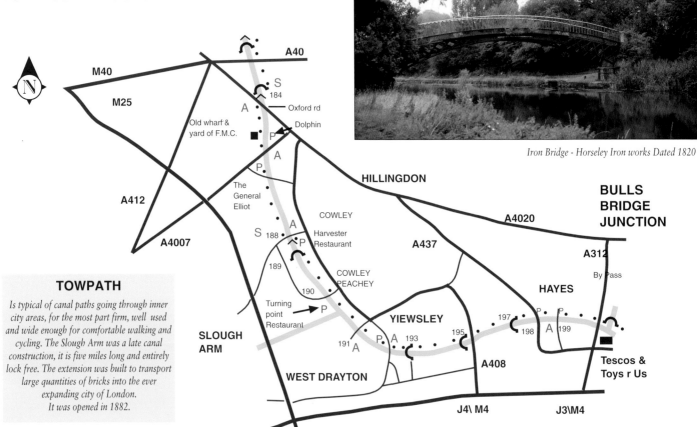

Iron Bridge - Horseley Iron works Dated 1820

M40

M25

A40

S
184

Oxford rd

Dolphin

Old wharf & yard of F.M.C.

A412

A4007

The General Elliot

COWLEY

Harvester Restaurant

HILLINGDON

A4020

BULLS BRIDGE JUNCTION

A312

By Pass

S 188

COWLEY PEACHEY

A437

HAYES

189

190

Turning point Restaurant

YIEWSLEY

197

198

199

TOWPATH

Is typical of canal paths going through inner city areas, for the most part firm, well used and wide enough for comfortable walking and cycling. The Slough Arm was a late canal construction, it is five miles long and entirely lock free. The extension was built to transport large quantities of bricks into the ever expanding city of London.
It was opened in 1882.

SLOUGH ARM

191

193

195

A408

WEST DRAYTON

J4\ M4

J3\M4

Tescos & Toys r Us

If you happen to live in the south, then this page may very well mark the start of your grand tour of the GRAND UNION CANAL and there is easy access between the two pubs indicated on Brentford High st. However, if like me you have worked your way south, then this is your final destination, and all I can say is well done, though don't expect to have a band playing when you arrive. I must admit I was worn out after four days of cycling down from Warwick, and I sat down by the bridge to check over my notes for the last few miles, and wait for my wife to come and rescue me in the car. On the way back up the motorway it was wonderful to relax into a comfortable car seat as we left Brentford behind and sped toward sunny Brum, and I started to savour the many fascinating aspects of my journey along The Grand Union. I loved the decorative iron turnover bridge just a mile or so out of Brentford (see photo) and stamped 1820. The Horseley Iron Works in Tipton used to be a massive place and for over one hundred and fifty years they produced thousands of canal and rail bridges for home and abroad. My father worked there during the seventies, but now it has been completely razed and replaced by a new housing estate. The situation reminds me of a verse from the Bible which says that the scene of this world is constantly changing (1stCor 7v1) and that is certainly true these days with new roads and housing estates springing up all over the place, to the extent that a whole neighbourhood can change it's appearance in just a decade. Fortunately some things change little over a hundred year span, and they help to give us a feeling of security in this crazy world, and the Grand Union is one of them. Windmill Bridge (205, the railway bridge) was designed in 1859 by Isambard Kingdom Brunel.

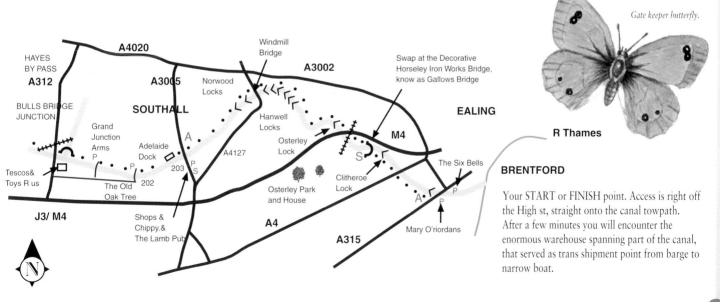

Gate keeper butterfly.

R Thames

BRENTFORD

Your START or FINISH point. Access is right off the High st, straight onto the canal towpath. After a few minutes you will encounter the enormous warehouse spanning part of the canal, that served as trans shipment point from barge to narrow boat.

THE OXFORD CANAL NAPTON JUNCTION TO OXFORD VIA BANBURY

All cyclable, but the centre section does have a poor towpath. 53 miles

There are many ways of exploring Oxfordshire to taste its varied delights, but to my mind the canal provides the finest avenue by far. Opening in the January of 1790 the Oxford being a fairly early waterway exhibits a constantly meandering course, as it keeps to a level by following the contour lines.This demonstrates without a doubt that the people in those not to distant times were not in the same sort of hurry to get places as we seem to be today. And that I suppose is the secret of its charm. Just being on the side of the canal takes us out of the fast lane and drops us gently into the slowest of all. If we take a look at the map for instance around Marston Doles, we can see that the distance from this village to Claydon as the crow flies is approximately five and a half miles, but the wandering Oxford doubles that to just over ten.

The Oxford has for some years now been a considerable hit with the narrowboating fraternity, but recently with improvements to the towpath, walkers and cyclists are discovering this

wonderful route, and the tranquillity that seems to ooze from its banks. Since its launch in 1995 as an official walk, British waterways have worked hard to clear whole sections of the towpath and lay a rather bright orange gravel,which will bed down with time and use. This improvement work however is on the Northern and Southern sections, and the middle is still as it was a hundred years ago, and though perfectly adequate for walking it is a little rough on the rear end for cyclists. Still this little problem can be easily overcome (if you have loads of money to spare) by kitting yourself out with a bike having front and rear suspension. Failing that, you can always ask your friendly dentist to give you an anaesthetic in the backside, the result is the same. Having said that, I cycled the whole length without suspension and enjoyed every mile. It was a gorgeous summer morning when my wife dropped me off near Napton Junction, and the access is from junction 12 of the M40, across to Southam, where you take the A425 for Napton on the

Hill. Then turn left when you reach the Murco garage, the Marina and canal are only a short distance down this narrow country lane. Of course its not necessary to go back to the canal junction to make a start, as it does entail a little back tracking, but the junction is attractive and it seems a shame to miss it out. As a matter of fact it was the day that new Labour took the governmental reins (remember that) so it was a new dawn for both of us, as I retraced my steps and made my way south along the twisting ribbon of water toward Banbury.

NOTES

1ST LEG The towpath between Napton junction and Banbury (23 miles) though narrow in places, is generally quite good, and there are plenty of access points, pubs and pretty villages on the way. The scenery is lush rolling farmland providing splendid opportunities for photography or sketching 2nd LEG. BANBURY is a large port of call, and has everything the traveller could want, after that its

back to small villages, and the whole of this area is worthy of further exploration though the towpath is poor. 3rd LEG Lower Heyford to Oxford. Pigeons lock to Oxford is definitely one of the best bits, great for families, having a good firm towpath with plenty of pubs en route to break up the journey and provide the necessary sustenance.

Chaffinch.

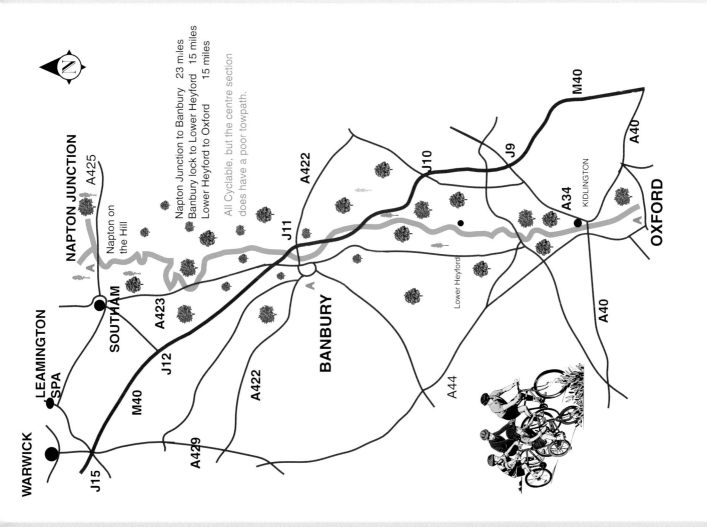

WARWICK

LEAMINGTON SPA

NAPTON JUNCTION

A425

Napton on the Hill

NAPTON JUNCTION to Banbury 23 miles
Banbury lock to Lower Heyford 15 miles
Lower Heyford to Oxford 15 miles

All Cyclable, but the centre section does have a poor towpath.

A422

J11

A423

SOUTHAM

J12

M40

A422

A429

J15

BANBURY

A44

A422

Lower Heyford

J10

J9

M40

A34

KIDLINGTON

A40

OXFORD

A40

33

NAPTON JUNCTION TO BANBURY LOCK
23 miles 22 locks. + Circular Routes via Priors Hardwick

TOWPATH

This map is a marvellous introduction to the Oxfordshire countryside. The towpath from Napton J, to Marston Doles varies greatly in width and surface, but from M/Doles to Claydon it has been given an orange gravel surface, a little soft for cycling but it will improve with time as it beds down.

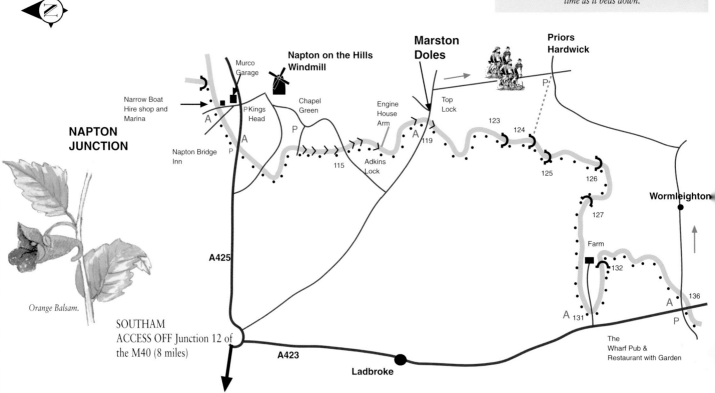

Napton on the Hills Windmill

Marston Doles

Priors Hardwick

Murco Garage

Narrow Boat Hire shop and Marina

NAPTON JUNCTION

P Kings Head

Chapel Green

Engine House Arm

Top Lock

123

124

A

A 119

Napton Bridge Inn

P

P

115

Adkins Lock

125

126

Wormleighton

127

Farm

132

136

A 131

A

P

A425

SOUTHAM
ACCESS OFF Junction 12 of the M40 (8 miles)

Orange Balsam.

A423

Ladbroke

The Wharf Pub & Restaurant with Garden

34

Napton Junction.

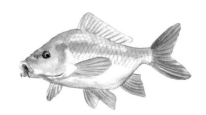

Carp. Can grow to huge sizes up to 1.5m and 35kg. Life span up to 50 years. Can be seen in spawning time, May-June, breaking surface of water, feeds on insects, and small crustacean.

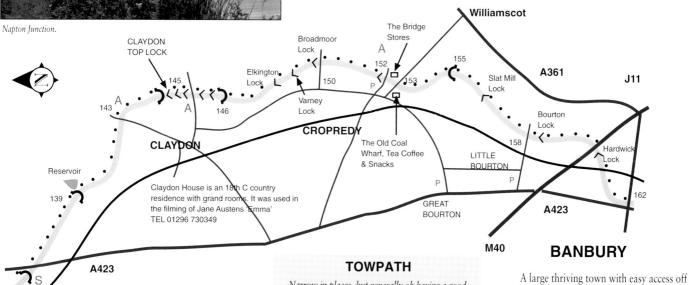

Williamscot

The Bridge Stores

Broadmoor Lock

CLAYDON TOP LOCK

Elkington Lock

152

155

Slat Mill Lock

A361

J11

145

150

153

146

Varney Lock

A

143

A

P

Bourton Lock

CROPREDY

158

Hardwick Lock

CLAYDON

The Old Coal Wharf, Tea Coffee & Snacks

LITTLE BOURTON

Reservoir

139

Claydon House is an 18th C country residence with grand rooms. It was used in the filming of Jane Austens 'Emma' TEL 01296 730349

P

P

GREAT BOURTON

162

A423

M40

BANBURY

S

137

A423

TOWPATH

Narrow in places, but generally ok having a good firm surface. Cropredy is a delightful sleepy little village. The Bridge Stores is a useful place to stock up your depleting supplies, and they have a wide range of groceries.

A large thriving town with easy access off junction 11 of the M40. Banbury has regular bus and train services.

COWROAST
Shop and Marina

FENNY COMPTON

P

BANBURY LOCK TO LOWER HEYFORD
15 miles 8 locks. + Circular Routes

The roads on this map are eminently cyclable, though a little hilly, and make alternative or circular routes as desired. Why not check out some of the villages ie Steeple Aston and Kings Sutton, the latters church which can be seen from the canal several miles away, as it sits on a gentle rise amidst a belt of trees.

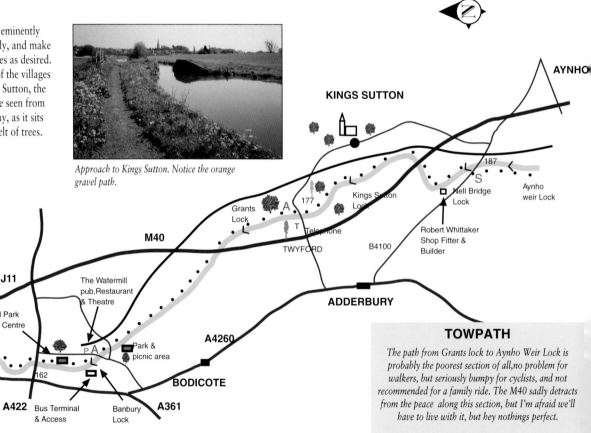

Approach to Kings Sutton. Notice the orange gravel path.

AYNHO

KINGS SUTTON

187

L
S

Aynho weir Lock

Nell Bridge Lock

Robert Whittaker Shop Fitter & Builder

Kings Sutton Lock

177

Grants Lock

A

T   Telephone

TWYFORD

B4100

M40

ADDERBURY

J11

The Watermill pub, Restaurant & Theatre

A4260

Spiceball Park & leisure Centre

P A

Park & picnic area

L

162

BODICOTE

A422

Bus Terminal & Access

Banbury Lock

A361

BANBURY

TOWPATH

The path from Grants lock to Aynho Weir Lock is probably the poorest section of all, no problem for walkers, but seriously bumpy for cyclists, and not recommended for a family ride. The M40 sadly detracts from the peace along this section, but I'm afraid we'll have to live with it, but hey nothings perfect.

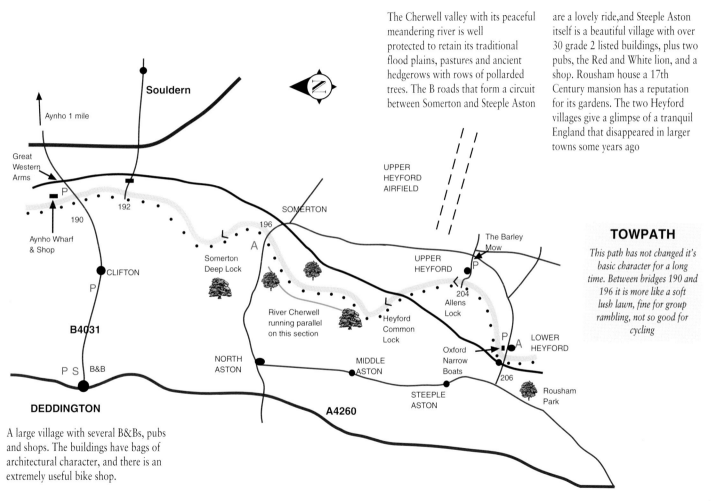

The Cherwell valley with its peaceful meandering river is well protected to retain its traditional flood plains, pastures and ancient hedgerows with rows of pollarded trees. The B roads that form a circuit between Somerton and Steeple Aston are a lovely ride, and Steeple Aston itself is a beautiful village with over 30 grade 2 listed buildings, plus two pubs, the Red and White lion, and a shop. Rousham house a 17th Century mansion has a reputation for its gardens. The two Heyford villages give a glimpse of a tranquil England that disappeared in larger towns some years ago

Souldern

Aynho 1 mile

Great Western Arms

P

Aynho Wharf & Shop

190

192

CLIFTON

P

B4031

P S   B&B

DEDDINGTON

A large village with several B&Bs, pubs and shops. The buildings have bags of architectural character, and there is an extremely useful bike shop.

SOMERTON

196

L

A

Somerton Deep Lock

River Cherwell running parallel on this section

L

Heyford Common Lock

NORTH ASTON

MIDDLE ASTON

STEEPLE ASTON

A4260

UPPER HEYFORD AIRFIELD

The Barley Mow

P

UPPER HEYFORD

204 Allens Lock

Oxford Narrow Boats

P   A

LOWER HEYFORD

206

Rousham Park

TOWPATH

This path has not changed it's basic character for a long time. Between bridges 190 and 196 it is more like a soft lush lawn, fine for group rambling, not so good for cycling

LOWER HEYFORD TO OXFORD
15 miles 9 locks.

TOWPATH

The towpath changes considerably as you go north from Pigeons Lock and becomes decidedly lumpy and bumpy. To compensate though the scene is extremely tranquil as the canal meanders through secluded leafy woodland, filled only with birdsong

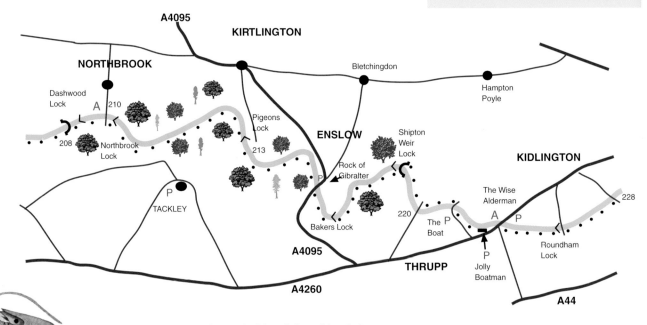

A4095

KIRTLINGTON

NORTHBROOK

Bletchingdon

Dashwood
Lock

A 210

Hampton
Poyle

208

Northbrook
Lock

Pigeons
Lock

ENSLOW

Shipton
Weir
Lock

213

KIDLINGTON

Rock of
Gibralter

P

The Wise
Alderman

228

P

TACKLEY

220

The P
Boat

A P

Roundham
Lock

Bakers Lock

A4095

THRUPP

P

Jolly
Boatman

A4260

A44

European Crayfish. Is a fresh water lobster that hunts small aquatic animals at night eg snails, worms also eats algae and moss. Up to 10cm in length, can live up to 12 years. They need good clean water to survive. Although nocturnal, crayfish maybe best seen in daylight at mating times in Oct and Nov.

TOWPATH

Is excellent from the very start of the canal at Hythe Bridge st. some eleven or twelve miles as far as Pigeons Lock. The path is wide and firm enough for family walking and cycling.So make the most of it, because after that it becomes somewhat harder going.

Roach. Occurs in all rivers and stagnant water in central and northern europe. Length 15-35cm, weight sometimes over 1kg. Spawns near bank in April-May. Lives on plants, small crustacean and insects.

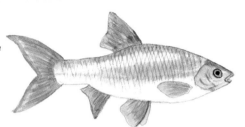

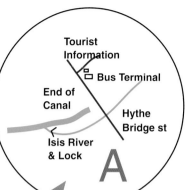

Tourist Information

Bus Terminal

End of Canal

Hythe Bridge st

Isis River & Lock

A

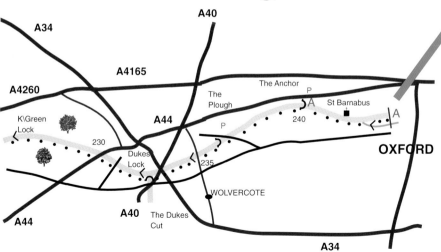

A34

A40

A4165

A4260

The Anchor

The Plough

A44

St Barnabus

K\Green Lock

230

Dukes Lock

235

240

OXFORD

A

A40

The Dukes Cut

WOLVERCOTE

A44

A34

Oxford has got to be one of Britains most exciting cities, having a rich history including the oldest university. Many of the colleges are open to visitors and there is a wealth of architectural interest. The information centre will tell you where to go and what to look for.

THE KENNET AND AVON CANAL AND THE BRISTOL TO BATH CYCLE PATH

READING TO WOOLHAMPTON	12 MILES	DEVIZES TO TROWBRIDGE	10 MILES
WOOLHAMPTON TO KINTBURY	13 MILES	TROWBRIDGE TO BATH	13 MILES
KINTBURY TO WOOTTON RIVERS	15 MILES	BATH TO BRISTOL	15 MILES
WOOTTON RIVERS TO DEVIZES	15 MILES	TOTAL 93 MILES (78) CANAL MILES APPROX	

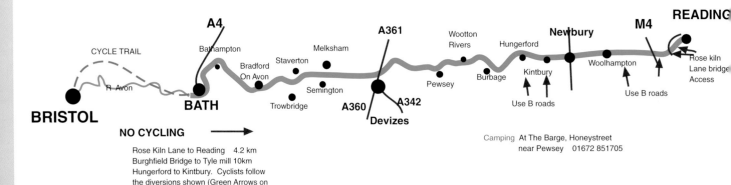

NO CYCLING

Rose Kiln Lane to Reading   4.2 km
Burghfield Bridge to Tyle mill 10km
Hungerford to Kintbury. Cyclists follow
the diversions shown (Green Arrows on
individual page maps)

Camping At The Barge, Honeystreet
        near Pewsey   01672 851705

The K&A today serves us as a beautiful linear park and nature trail, stretching for over seventy miles through a predominantly rural landscape, that includes farmland, meadows, woodland, river valleys and stunning chalk vales that provide an amazing variety of habitats for flora and fauna. The canal itself is actually made up of three waterways (River Kennet in the East, River Avon in the West, and canal in the middle.) tied cleverly together by the engineer John Rennie in 1810 to carry agricultural goods and the stuff of the industrial revolution, coal iron and stone. For the next thirty or forty years the canal proved to be the mode of transport for heavy goods between London and Bristol, but after the construction of the Great Western Railway in 1841 trade rapidly moved over to the much faster goods train. From then on the condition of the canal gradually declined, and by world war two it was truly derelict. Thankfully not everyone wanted to see this marvellous waterway disappear, and the Kennet and Avon Trust was formed to champion it's cause. A huge amount of work was however required to bring the canal back to it's former glory, and the Trust along with British Waterways set about the task. Finally in 1990 the necessary work was complete, the Queen came along to do the honours, and the K&A navigation was open once more from Reading to Bristol. The job was not finished however and the partnership was reformed to request help from the lottery. In 1996 a grant of £25 million was agreed securing the future of the waterway.

I seem to pick notable dates when doing my canal reconnaissance trips, and this one turned out to be no exception. As I headed south on the M40 with my wife, heading for Reading and a pale blue sky we turned on the radio at 7-15 to hear the tragic news of the car accident involving Diana, Princess of Wales and her subsequent death. It required no special prophetic spirit on my part to predict what the weeks media would be filled with, and sure enough that's how it went. That evening I pitched my little tent somewhere near Kintbury (the exact location is still a secret) and made my way along to the village pub for a meal and a drink. Even the pub seemed strangely connected with the days events, being called The Prince of Wales, and as I tucked into my chicken dinner it was fascinating to listen to the locals voice their opinions on what had happened

My attention was forced however onto the days travel, and the notes and photographs that had been taken, and I covered the table with maps, leaflets and odd bits of paper. As a visitor from the midlands with an obvious interest in canals, and the Kennet and Avon in particular, I had heard much about the proposed £15 cycling permit from a variety of sources. This permit scheme was being trialled by British Waterways on the Kennet and Avon with the possibility of extending it nationwide. Perhaps because of all the attention being given to this canal in the connection with cycling it had led to great expectations on my part. I was however in for a bit of a disappointment as I covered the first twenty five miles and came to the same conclusion as BW, that much of this section near to Reading was unsuitable for comfortable cycling.

> 66 *My advice for cyclists however is start at Newbury and work your way West, as the towpath is better from this point on, and only start at Reading if you are determined to do the whole canal from end to end. But be prepared to make the necessary diversions where British Waterways direct (see main map) Opposite.* 99

At Southcote lock I had encountered a metal barrier to deter cyclists from crossing a bridge, and there were several stiles to climb over when passing from one field to the next.

Fortunately the weather had been kind to me that day and I had basked in warm sunshine, as for the nettles, that was another thing. Have you noticed how the little blighters always grow into the path and never away from it? I could almost hear them calling to each other as I approached ' Look lads, he's only got shorts on, lets whack him across the legs as he goes by'. And so it was, that I went to bed that night with gently throbbing knees and shins. The next day my luck turned, and to my amazement I actually found a five pound note on the towpath, and there wasn't a soul for miles. Now I'm the sort of person that goes through life losing things not finding them, so this came a bit of a shock to the system. I had ridden over the folded note when something deep in the recesses of my brain had sprung to life and operated the brakes. I slid to a halt, went back a few yards to picked up my prize, and it was with great glee that I purchased a free meal in Wootton Rivers that day. The pub in question was The Royal Oak, it was extremely old, as is the village, and I sat outside with my ploughmans lunch (which came to a fiver exactly) and listened to the "frightfully clear' accents of middle England

It was on the second or third day that I noticed the similarity between the K&A and the LLangollen canal. Each waterway has it's start in a modest setting, and them improves markedly with every mile that you travel west. So my advice for towpath travellers is start at Reading and head for the setting sun, not only does the towpath improve but so does the scenery, the villages and towns that you pass through. So on I went, visiting Newbury, Devizes,, Bradford on Avon and enjoying equally the smaller places in-between.

Kingfisher.

THE BRISTOL AND BATH RAILWAY CYCLE TRAIL

14 miles plus 1.5 miles to the start of the canal

ACCESS

The start\ finish of the trail is well sign posted in Bristol. It is found off St Philips road, which is actually on a trading estate on the East side of the city.

MANGOTSFIELD
Staple Hill Tunnel
Teewell Hill
Soundwell rd
Sistons Hill
Filwood rd
Lodge Causeway
Ridgeway rd
WARMLEY
Public Toilets
A420
KINGSWOOD
High st
London rd
LAWRENCE HILL
BRISTOL
TEMPLE MEADS
ST ANNES PARK
A431
N
Cherry Garden Lane
BITTON STATION
AVON WALKWAY
OLDLAND
A4
A4175
KEYNSHAM

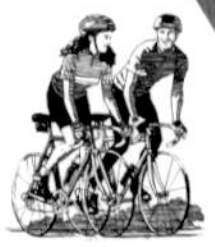

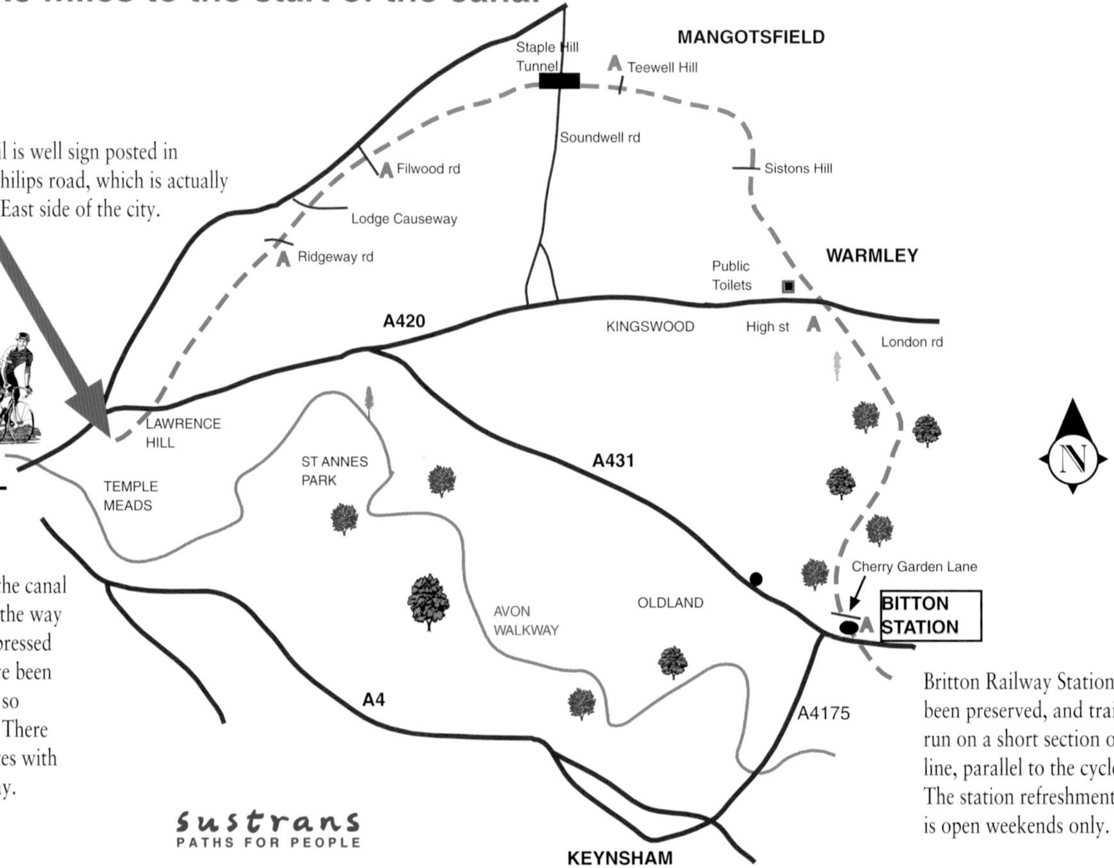

If Birmingham is the centre of the canal world then Bristol surely leads the way for cycling, and I was most impressed with the arrangements that have been made over the last ten years or so to make the city cycle friendly. There are plenty of well marked routes with little blue signs pointing the way.

sustrans
PATHS FOR PEOPLE

Britton Railway Station ha been preserved, and trains run on a short section of t line, parallel to the cycle tr The station refreshment ro is open weekends only.

Could the builders of this railway with it's high embankments and numerous bridges ever have envisioned it being turned into a route for cyclists and walkers, I think not, but that is exactly what has happened here in between Bath and Bristol. Now at the end of the twentieth century it's good to see the trail full of life with two wheeled commuters and pleasure cyclists alike. For 95% of the journey the surface is superb smooth tarmac, making it suitable for wheelchair users. The trail was constructed in stages between 1979 and 1986, and it's Bristol start point at St Philips road is marked with a large timber framed gateway, that has been carved to commemorate ' Cycle Bags' the Bristol based cycle campaign group, who were the original motivating force for the scheme. The work was carried out by the local council (well done) and Sustrans. The route is generally level, but there is a gentle climb up and out of Bristol towards Fishponds, and the views across the city are pretty good. The Bird In Hand is easily accessed off the viaduct, and the Jolly Sailor is a couple of minutes down the lane where you can get a delicious meal overlooking the river.

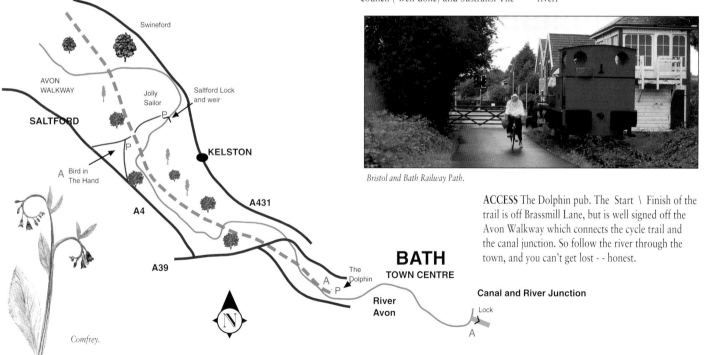

Bristol and Bath Railway Path.

ACCESS The Dolphin pub. The Start \ Finish of the trail is off Brassmill Lane, but is well signed off the Avon Walkway which connects the cycle trail and the canal junction. So follow the river through the town, and you can't get lost - - honest.

Canal and River Junction

BATH TO TOWBRIDGE(KINGS ARMS)
13 miles

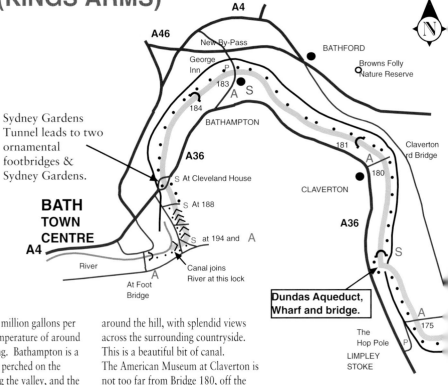

Sydney Gardens Tunnel leads to two ornamental footbridges & Sydney Gardens.

BATH TOWN CENTRE

A4

River

At Foot Bridge

A

S At Cleveland House

S At 188

S at 194 and

Canal joins River at this lock

A

A4

New By-Pass

George Inn

P

183

A S

184

BATHAMPTON

A36

BATHFORD

Browns Folly Nature Reserve

181

A

Claverton rd Bridge

180

CLAVERTON

A36

S

Dundas Aqueduct, Wharf and bridge.

175

A

P

The Hop Pole

LIMPLEY STOKE

N

Bath is a city known nationally and internationally for it's history, architecture and natural hot springs. The Romans called it Aque-Sulis, and built amongst other things a temple to their goddess Sulis Minerva. The Romans were however only capitilizing on the springs that others before them had also used for therapeutic purposes, (it probably made them feel good as well) After the Romans came the Normans and then the Georgians, who in the 18th century built all the posh houses, and turned the whole town into a holiday come health resort, a kind of ye old Centre Parks.

The hot springs still flow today, 2000 years after the Romans, at an impressive quarter million gallons per day, at a steady temperature of around 46 degrees, amazing. Bathampton is a very pretty village, perched on the hillside overlooking the valley, and the cottages seem to have lined themselves up in readiness for the passing photographer.

Cyclists, make the most of the super towpath as it winds its way around the hill, with splendid views across the surrounding countryside. This is a beautiful bit of canal. The American Museum at Claverton is not too far from Bridge 180, off the A36. Claverton Pumping Station, open to visitors, still operates its original pump on selected days in the summer. Warleigh Manor can be seen across the valley.

The Avoncliff and Dundas aqueducts, both on this superb section of canal, were the technical achievements of the day, and are still visited and admired for their architectural magnificence. If you look at the Avoncliff carefully you will notice a definite sag in the middle of the stonework, but don't worry it has received a concrete lining to give it strength. Bradford on Avon is definitely worthy of exploration, with it's interesting town centre and hillside terraced buildings, that gaze down toward the river below. The town gets it's name from 'the Broad Ford', which in medieval times was replaced by a stone bridge, and two of it's original 13th century arches are extant. The old winding streets of B on A are a pleasure to walk around, as is the nearby Tithe Barn and Saxon Church of St Laurence from about 700 AD.

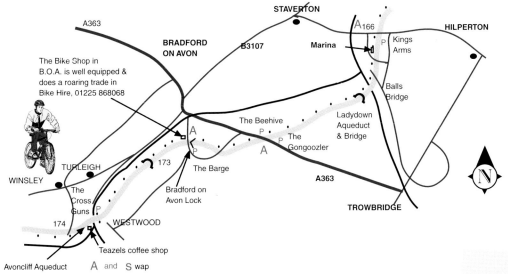

Common Blue.

TOWPATH

Is wide and well maintained, so if the skies are blue, and you are gently peddling your way along this particular section , you must be in cyclists heaven.
(Not bad for walkers either)

TROWBRIDGE TO DEVIZES
10 miles

The KENNET & AVON CANAL TRUST
This organisation has now been working
hard for many years to restore and
maintain this marvellous waterway for the
benefit of all. The work included 86
derelict locks, 344 rotting lock gates,
leaking canal beds and gently crumbling
aqueducts. Obviously therefore money and
help is always required, so if you feel you
can help in any way either pop into the
canal centre in Devizes, or ring
01380 721279.

Hog Iris

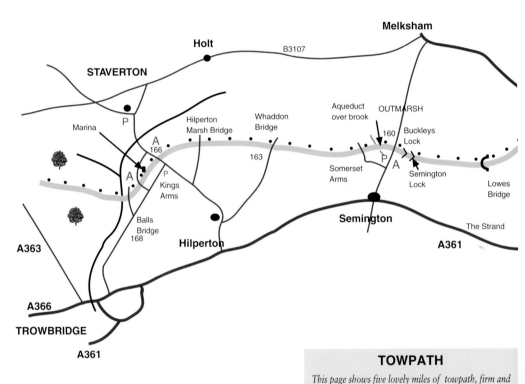

TOWPATH

*This page shows five lovely miles of towpath, firm and
wide enough for comfortable cycling. The Kings
Arms is only a few hundred yards from bridge 166.*

The TOWPATH on this section is gritted, rolled and well maintained, which only goes to show, you can always tell where the B.W. Manager resides. The Canal Museum in Devizes tells the history of the Kennet and Avon with pictures, and models in a large upstairs room, while downstairs there is a well stocked bookshop with gifts and souvenirs. 01380 729489. What a magnificent view this is of the surrounding countryside from the top of the Caen Hill flight of locks just west of Devizes. Completed in 1810, and restored for the 1990 re-opening, these 16 watery steps go straight down the hillside, and make an equally spectacular sight from the bottom. When viewed from below, each lock is seen to own its own small reservoir on the left. (No they are not terraced duck ponds)

Caen Hill flight of locks.

Gudgeon. Recognised by single barbel on either side of mouth and strikingly large fins. Lives at bottom of canal feeding on small animals and vegetable debris. Length 10-20cm.

47

DEVIZES TO WOOTTON RIVERS

15 miles + Circular Routes

TOWPATH

A central narrow track with grass on both sides

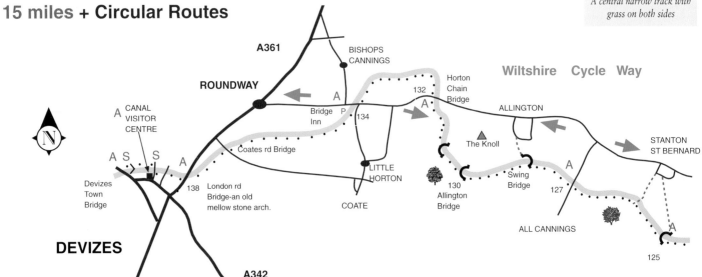

A361

BISHOPS CANNINGS

ROUNDWAY

Horton Chain Bridge

Wiltshire Cycle Way

132

A

CANAL VISITOR CENTRE

A

Bridge Inn

P

ALLINGTON

134

N

STANTON ST BERNARD

A   S   S   S   A

The Knoll

Coates rd Bridge

Devizes Town Bridge

LITTLE HORTON

130 Allington Bridge

Swing Bridge

A

138   London rd Bridge-an old mellow stone arch.

COATE

127

ALL CANNINGS

DEVIZES

A342

A360

125

I must admit that the Vale of Pewsey is one of the most stunningly beautiful regions I have ever had the privilege of setting my eyes on. It was the first week in September when I passed through, the fields had just been harvested and the grain was lying randomly around the fields either in the traditional

oblong bales, or in the more modern circular shapes. The road out of Devizes to Wootton Rivers is wonderful for cyclists, and can be utilised to create circular routes. The villages that lie on this trail are a photographers delight, with their thatched roofs and well tended gardens.

Allington on circular route.

ALLINGTON
Drive Carefully

48

A wonderfully tranquil, pretty section of the K&A. The area around the canal is mainly served by quieter B roads, and the normally present railway with it's continual noise has gone somewhere else. The towpath is generally grassy, with a central worn track, though quite firm. The surrounding countryside is full of undulating curves reminiscent of a reclining nude. The waterway winds it's way through this gently rolling landscape with it's strange conical hills, and bordered only by wild flowers and grain fields,which have been continually harvested for three thousand years or more. The decorative Ladies Bridge (120) was built to please Lady Wroughton who owned the land in the early 1800s. The canal was also widened to make it more attractive at the same spot.   The Vale of Pewsey separates Wiltshires two main areas of chalk, Salisbury plain in the South, and the Marlborough Downs to the North.

In Pewsey village at the crossroads there stands a statue of King Alfred who ruled over this area many years ago. The 700 year old church of St John the Baptist is built on a foundation of stones that the Saxons laid, and the ancient highway now known as The Ridgeway comes down to the canal just South East of Alton Barnes.

Wootton Rivers is a picturesque village with thatched roofs. The Royal Oak is a splendid large old pub, extremely posh.

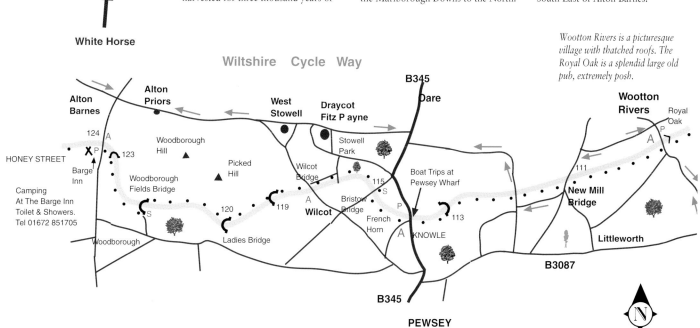

White Horse

Wiltshire   Cycle   Way

WOOTTON RIVERS TO KINTBURY
15 miles + Circular Route

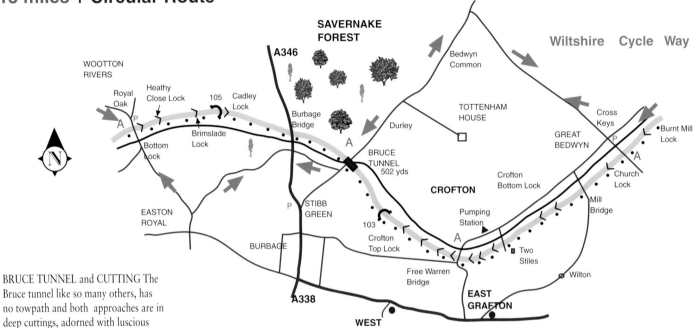

WOOTTON RIVERS

Royal Oak

Heathy Close Lock

105

Cadley Lock

Brimslade Lock

Bottom Lock

A346

SAVERNAKE FOREST

Burbage Bridge

Durley

BRUCE TUNNEL 502 yds

A

Bedwyn Common

TOTTENHAM HOUSE

CROFTON

Pumping Station

Crofton Bottom Lock

Wiltshire Cycle Way

Cross Keys

GREAT BEDWYN

Burnt Mill Lock

Church Lock

Mill Bridge

Two Stiles

Wilton

N

EASTON ROYAL

P

STIBB GREEN

BURBAGE

103

Crofton Top Lock

Free Warren Bridge

A338

WEST GRAFTON

EAST GRAFTON

BRUCE TUNNEL and CUTTING The Bruce tunnel like so many others, has no towpath and both approaches are in deep cuttings, adorned with luscious woodland on both banks. In the past, boats were hauled through by a chain that was fixed to the brick lined bore, while the horses were led over the top. And that's the way we are going to go, that is unless you fancy going for a swim in the dark. So simply follow the track over the top. If your travelling West it may appear that your suddenly heading for the railway, but don't worry there's a strange little tunnel to go through that leads right onto the canal side.

TOWPATH
A mile or so East of Wootton Rivers it is rolled and gritted (Great Stuff), After Burbage bridge it is narrow with a central track, but ok. Between Crofton Top lock and Church lock it is much wider, with much of it having been widened and smoothed. East of Church Lock it is grass but firm.

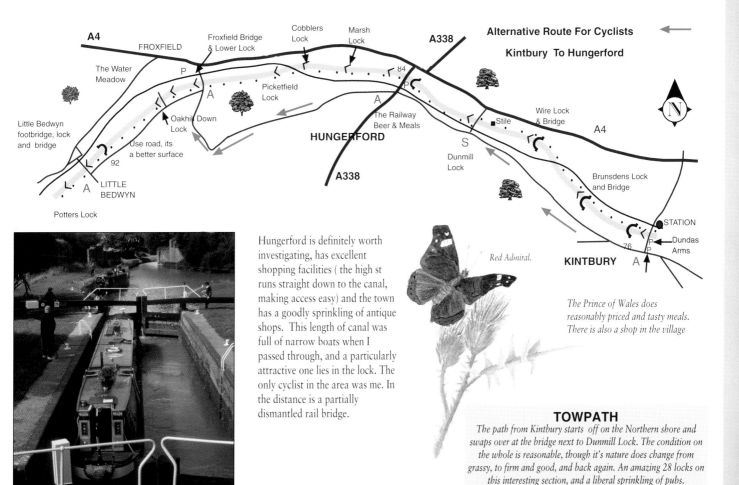

A4

FROXFIELD

The Water Meadow

Froxfield Bridge & Lower Lock

Cobblers Lock

Marsh Lock

A338

Picketfield Lock

P

A

Little Bedwyn footbridge, lock and bridge

Oakhill Down Lock

Use road, its a better surface

92

L

A

LITTLE BEDWYN

Potters Lock

84

P

A

HUNGERFORD

The Railway Beer & Meals

A338

S

Dunmill Lock

Stile

Wire Lock & Bridge

A4

N

Brunsdens Lock and Bridge

STATION

76

P P

Dundas Arms

KINTBURY

A

Red Admiral.

Hungerford is definitely worth investigating, has excellent shopping facilities (the high st runs straight down to the canal, making access easy) and the town has a goodly sprinkling of antique shops. This length of canal was full of narrow boats when I passed through, and a particularly attractive one lies in the lock. The only cyclist in the area was me. In the distance is a partially dismantled rail bridge.

Crofton Top Lock, the last one in a flight of seven.

The Prince of Wales does reasonably priced and tasty meals. There is also a shop in the village

TOWPATH
The path from Kintbury starts off on the Northern shore and swaps over at the bridge next to Dunmill Lock. The condition on the whole is reasonable, though it's nature does change from grassy, to firm and good, and back again. An amazing 28 locks on this interesting section, and a liberal sprinkling of pubs.

KINTBURY VIA NEWBURY TO WOOLHAMPTON
13 miles 17 locks. + Circular routes

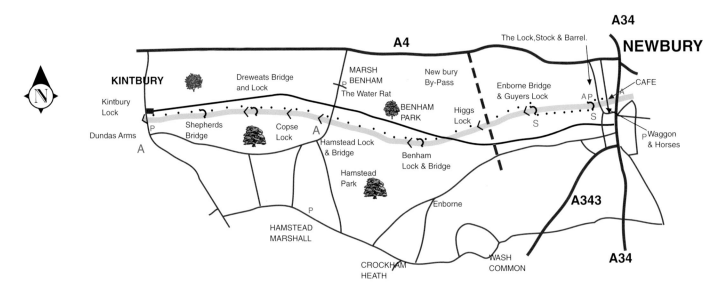

The Dundas Arms, like the Dundas Aqueduct is named after Charles Dundas, Baron of Amesbury, who was involved with the canal during its construction, and actually presided over the complete opening in 1810. The first section to be opened however was the stretch between Kintbury and Newbury in 1797. Newbury has an elegant town bridge that wouldn't look out of place in Venice, though there is no towpath under it, and travellers need to do a minor diversion by crossing the road. There are horse drawn boat trips to be had at Kintbury, and don't forget that the railway runs parallel to this section and can be utilised for one way walking.

TOWPATH
Good path between Newbury and Higgs Lock, narrow and poor between Higgs Lock and Hamstead Lock, then there is a short piece around Dreweats Bridge that gets a little muddy after rain, and after that it improves again up to Kintbury. Work was progressing well on the By Pass during my trip, so I guessed that Swampy and his friends had failed in their attempt to prevent this particular development. It is represented by a dotted red line just East of Higgs Lock. The B roads via Crockham Heath, and Hamstead Marshal make fine circular routes.

Thatcham now has a Nature Discovery Centre where visitors
are encouraged to use their senses on a range of activities.

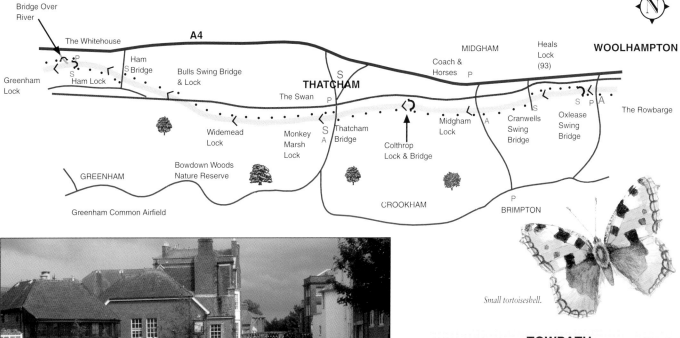

Bridge Over River

The Whitehouse

A4

MIDGHAM

Heals Lock (93)

WOOLHAMPTON

Coach & Horses

Greenham Lock

Ham Lock

Ham Bridge

Bulls Swing Bridge & Lock

THATCHAM

The Swan

Widemead Lock

Monkey Marsh Lock

Thatcham Bridge

Colthrop Lock & Bridge

Midgham Lock

Cranwells Swing Bridge

Oxlease Swing Bridge

The Rowbarge

GREENHAM

Bowdown Woods Nature Reserve

Greenham Common Airfield

CROOKHAM

BRIMPTON

Small tortoiseshell.

TOWPATH

*This is one of those sections that exhibits a range of towpath
conditions. Woolhampton to Midgham Lock it is mainly grass, but
firm, with gravel in places. Then there is one mile of poor path (muddy
after rain) up to Colthrop Lock, and then it improves considerably all
the way to Greenham Lock. The River Kennet puts in an occasional
appearance as it winds an East-West course just South of the Canal.
Circular routes via Brimpton, Crookham and Greenham.*

Newbury lock.

WOOLHAMPTON TO READING

12 miles

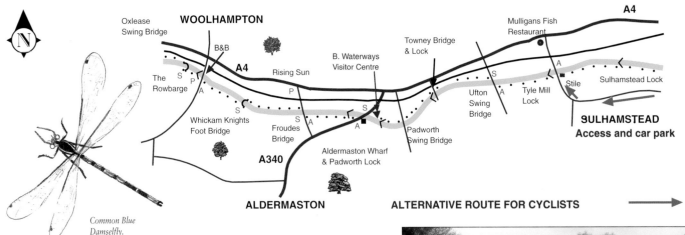

Common Blue Damselfly.

Bridge Cottage at Woolhampton is a delightful B&B, Timber framed with brick infil.(17 century) It is only a few yards from the towpath. Tel 0118 9713138. The A4 is about 150 metres away as is a small shop. Aldermaston Lock with it's unique and artistic scalloped brickwork on the internal walls. The swing bridge in the background is lights controlled, they are an interesting feature of the K&A and must be operated with care. Photo of typical towpath on this section. Notice the heavy foliage growing at the waters edge. (picture on opposite page)

ALTERNATIVE ROUTE FOR CYCLISTS ➔

Aldermaston lock.

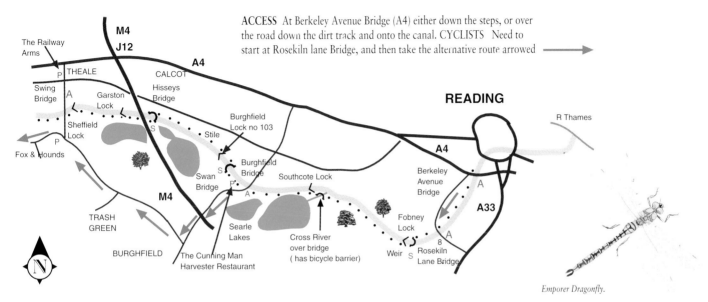

ACCESS At Berkeley Avenue Bridge (A4) either down the steps, or over the road down the dirt track and onto the canal. CYCLISTS Need to start at Rosekiln lane Bridge, and then take the alternative route arrowed ⟶

M4
J12

The Railway Arms

THEALE

A4

CALCOT

Swing Bridge

Garston Lock

Hisseys Bridge

READING

R Thames

Sheffield Lock

Burghfield Lock no 103

Stile

Fox & Hounds

Burghfield Bridge

Swan Bridge

Southcote Lock

Berkeley Avenue Bridge

M4

A4

A33

TRASH GREEN

Searle Lakes

Fobney Lock

BURGHFIELD

The Cunning Man Harvester Restaurant

Cross River over bridge (has bicycle barrier)

Weir

Rosekiln Lane Bridge

N

Emporer Dragonfly.

The canal, River Kennet, railway and A4 are constant travelling companions for this leg of the journey. Fortunately the railway with it's noisy trains keeps it's distance, but it can come in useful for one way walking or cycling. During the summer of 1997 British Waterways decided to run a pilot scheme for cycling along the Kennet and Avon canal, thus demonstrating that they are trying to get to grips with making much better use of the towpaths. This map however contains two of the three small sections that BW want cyclists to avoid because of having poor towpaths, and I must admit that I agree with them, plus the fact that I encountered other obstacles along the way in the shape of stiles which need to be clambered over.

The Kennet and Avon makes it's start by a junction with the Thames, but there are difficulties in following the canal through the city, so my advice is not to try, but commence at Berkeley Ave Bridge, and go South West.

THE CHANGING ROLE OF BRITAINS CANALS

The popularity of cruising Britains canals in a narrow boat has increased greatly over the last thirty years, and continues on a steady upward curve, with a similar rising demand for new and secondhand boats, marinas and boating paraphernalia

Now at the end of the nineties, thousands of individuals live permanently on their own boat, while thousands more from home and abroad, hire a boat for a week or more for their annual holidays. The canals however have much more potential for leisure, and many waterway enthusiasts have seen the possibility of using the towpaths for creating equally popular long distance cycling and walking routes. Even wheelchair users could take advantage of these paths if the surface was made smooth enough (which it is in places)

Back in 1985 canal author Roger Squires, in his book 'Canal Walks' put forward a perfect case for towpath improvements, even using drawings to illustrate what could be done to produce a good quality towpath. He noted that the countryside commission were also making similar

recommendations. Personally I believe that cycling is an absolutely marvellous way to travel the canal network, and doesn't have the disadvantage of having to lock up or down. Generally speaking the towpaths are on flat ground and suit cyclists of all ages, especially those getting on in years. Sustrans, the cycling charity organisation has already invested money in certain areas of canal towpath as they seek to create thousands of miles of off road cycle lanes for the millennium, and the fourteen miles between Birmingham and Wolverhampton is a prime example. Though it must be admitted that not all of this path has been done, and much of the financial help came from the local councils. Infact as I write, Sandwell Council is planning to spend a lot more money on it's own towpath improvements. This all goes to show that the role of the canal in society has drastically changed since its origination, and maybe we are entering a third canal era? It is of course heartening to see that British Waterways, Local authorities and canal societies with their splendid volunteers, are all working to enhance

these routes. Sadly not everyone is in favour of these changes, and some individuals are even opposed to improving the towpaths and thus seeing more cyclists on them. Therefore I would encourage this concerned minority to visit the Kennet and Avon, somewhere between Bradford on Avon and Bath to see what can be achieved.

There has been some wonderful work done on this particular stretch, and the path is wide with a smooth and gritted surface, making it possible for all canal users to enjoy the route in harmony. Above is the Bradford on Avon bike shop, which is perfectly situated on the side of the canal, and does a brisk trade in cycle hire.

USEFUL INFORMATION

TOURIST INFORMATION CENTRES

READING	The Town Hall, Blagrave st,	
	Reading. RG1 1QH .	0118 956 6226
BRISTOL	St Nicholas Church,St	
	Nicholas st, Bristol.	0117 9260767
DEVIZES	Crown Centre, 39 St John st,	
	Devizes	01380 729408
BRADFORD ON AVON	34 Silver st, Bradford on Avon	01225 865797
BATH	Abbey Chambers, Abbey	
	Church Yard. Bath	01225 462831
BIRMINGHAM	Convention & Visitor Bureaux	
	2 City Arcade, Birmingham	0121 6432514

MUSEUMS & GALLERIES

The Museum of Reading, Blagrave st, Reading	01189 939 9800
History and Development of Reading.	
From Saxon to modern times.	
Roman Baths Museum and Pump Room	
Abbey Church Yard, Bath	01225 477785
Victoria Art Gallery. Bridge st, Bath	01225 477772
Stoke Bruerne Canal Museum	01604 862229
Blakes Lock Museum, Gasworks rd , Reading	0118 9390918
Industrial Heritage & Exhibits	
Museum of Costume, Bennet st , Bath	
Bristol Industrial Museum.	
Princes Wharf, Wapping rd Bristol	0117 925 1470
Birmingham Museum of Science & Industry	
Newhall st , Birmingham.	0121 236 1022
Devizes Museum, 41 Long st, Devizes.	01380 727369
Bristol City Museum, Queens rd,Clifton,Bristol	0117 922 3571
Birmingham Museum and Art Gallery	
Chamberlain Square.	0121 235 2834

BRITISH WATERWAYS

Customer Services.	
Willow Grange, Church rd, Watford	01923 226081
Bath rd, Devizes, Wiltshire. SN101HB	01380 722859
Brome Hall Lane,Lapworth, Solihull	
West Midlands ,	01564 784634
The Stop House, Braunston, Northamptonshire	
NN117JQ	01788 890666
Marsworth Junction, Watery Lane, Marsworth, Tring,	
Hertfordshire, HP234LZ	01442 890648
Brindley House, Corner Hall, Lawn Lane,	
Hemel Hempstead, Herts, HP39YT.	01442 235400

BIKES AND CYCLE HIRE

Devizes Bikes, Cycle Hire. Pinecroft, Potterne rd	01380 721433
On Your Bike, 10 Priory Queensway,Birmingham.	0121 627 1590
Bruces Bikes. 12 Gloucester rd north,Filton, Bristol.	0117 9499941
M.J. Hiscock Cycles, 59 Northgate st,Devizes	01380 722236
Avon Valley Cycles. Arch 37, Rear of Bath Spa Station	01225 461880
Bradford On Avon Cycles.(Next to the Canal)	01225 868068

ACKNOWLEDGMENTS
Thanks to Jane for the artwork. British
Waterways for their help and all those who
posed for pictures.

NOTES:

WILDE'S CYCLE GUIDES

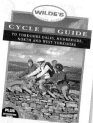

FULL COLOUR PHOTOGRAPHY•FULL COLOUR EASY TO FOLLOW MAPS•FULLY ILLUSTRATED THROUGHOUT•PLACES OF INTEREST

Wildes cycle Guides show a selection of the very best almost traffic free routes.

[1] Derbyshire, Cheshire & North Staffs.
[2] Lancashire and the Lakes
[3] Yorkshire Dales, Humberside, North and West Yorkshire.
[4] Devon, Cornwall and West Somerset.
[5] Norfolk, Suffolk and Essex.
[6] Grand Union, Oxford and Kennet and Avon Canals.
[7] Trail Quest A guide to trails for the walker, cyclist and disabled around North West Water land.

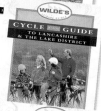

POSTAGE & PACKAGING FREE

These are not mountain rides but enjoyable journeys for the whole family to take at whatever pace and time they wish. Each route has its own map showing everything you need to know from distances and directions to parking, picnic and rest stops. Wildes Cycle Guides are available through bookshops, WH Smiths and selected cycle shops or by mail order from Gildersleve Publishing. (see address below)

BOUND FOR EASE OF USE•LAMINATED COVER FOR DURABILITY•HANDY A5 210MM x 148MM SIZE TO FIT HANDLE BAR BAG MAP CASE

Please send me.
Please tick where appropriate.

19 trails in Lancs and the Lakes	£6.75
35 trails in Derbyshire, Cheshire & N. Staffs	£8.99
50 trails in Norfolk Suffolk and Essex	£9.95
34 trails in Yorkshire and Humberside	£7.50
30 trails in Devon and Cornwall	£7.95
Grand Union, Oxford and Kennet and Avon Canals	£8.99
Trail Quest	£7.95

20% OFF when you buy two guides 30% OFF when you buy 3 or more

Name: ....

Address: ....

.... **Postcode:** ....

Payment: Credit card ☐   Cheque* ☐   Postal order ☐

Signature ....

Credit Card ☐☐☐☐☐☐☐☐☐☐☐☐☐☐☐☐   Expiry Date ☐☐☐☐

*Please make cheques payable to **Gildersleve Publishing Ltd.** Post Payment to:
Wilde's, 19 Water Street, Hapton, Burnley, Lancs. BB12 7LQ.

NOTES: